Cokie

Also by Steven V. Roberts

Eureka

From This Day Forward (with Cokie Roberts)

My Fathers' Houses

From Every End of This Earth

Our Haggadah (with Cokie Roberts)

Bethesda and Chevy Chase

Pawleys Island (with Lee G. Brockington)

Cokie

A LIFE WELL LIVED

STEVEN V. ROBERTS

HARPER

An Imprint of HarperCollins*Publishers*

HarperCollins books may be purchased for educational, business, or sales promotional use. For information, please email the Special Markets Department at SPsales@harpercollins.com.

Photo Credits: Donna Svennevik/©ABC/Getty Images (p. 1); Jack Howard (p. 53); NPR (p. 83); Steve Fenn/©ABC/Getty Images (p. 113); Roberts family photo (p. 145); Joseph Gidjunis/The Museum of the American Revolution (p. 187); Ian Wolverton/Save the Children (p. 221); Roberts family photo (p. 247)

FIRST EDITION

Designed by Leah Carlson-Stanisic

Library of Congress Cataloging-in-Publication Data has been applied for.

ISBN 978-0-06-285147-5

21 22 23 24 25   LSC   10 9 8 7 6 5 4 3 2 1

For Cokie,
The Love of My Life

Contents

Cokie

Introduction

"What Would Cokie Do?"

Cokie died on September 17, 2019, a week after we celebrated our 53rd wedding anniversary. When I gave a eulogy at her funeral in the Cathedral of St. Matthew the Apostle in downtown Washington, my aim was simply to tell stories—some funny, some poignant, all personal—to illustrate her truly remarkable life. There were a thousand mourners in the church that morning, but countless others heard the ceremony on TV, and the reactions I received were overwhelming. People were hungry for more stories about her—her origins and her impact, her generosity and her goodness. So that's why I decided to write this book.

Cokie lived much of her life in public, by the accident of her birth and the choice of her career. Her parents, Hale and Lindy Boggs, both served in Congress, representing the city of New

Orleans for a total of almost fifty years. The Speaker of the House, Sam Rayburn, was a frequent dinner guest during her childhood in the 1950s (in the home I still live in), and President and Mrs. Johnson came to our wedding in 1966 (in the garden of that home). Many obituaries referred to her as the ultimate "Washington insider," even as "Washington royalty," but her professional success flowed from her own tenacity and talent, not family connections. She wasn't a full-time journalist until she was thirty-four years old, but she made up for lost time, crashing through glass ceilings at NPR and ABC with her impressive mind, impish wit, and infectious laugh. "The laugh," wrote *Lear's* magazine, "distinguishes her from the self-important chin-tuggers of her trade, makes her someone people connect with." She loved hearing from young women who had followed her on the radio or watched her on TV or heard her at their school and said to themselves, "I can be Cokie Roberts. I can be that smart, that confident, that powerful." Diane Sawyer, a colleague at ABC and a fellow graduate of Wellesley, once said, "She made you brave."

In another way, however, she wasn't royalty at all. She was accessible and approachable, a "suburban housewife," as she often called herself, or an "everywoman," as she told *Lear's*: "People think I'm sort of sensible and like them and go to the grocery store and worry about tuition." But every woman didn't have her propensity for puncturing pomposity—especially if it came from a man, as it usually did. Me included. "Her ability to call foul on something that didn't make sense, it just endeared her to people," said ABC executive Bob Murphy. David Westin, who headed ABC News during much of Cokie's tenure there, put it this way: "She was just Cokie. She knew the stuff, she knew the material, she knew it better than everyone else. And she would tell you what she knew. But she also had, and it sounds lofty, a moral compass to her about right and wrong that she brought to her reporting that stopped short of moralizing." George Will, who shared ABC's Sunday-morning program with her for many years, mentioned Roone Arledge, who preceded Westin as head of ABC News and originally hired Cokie: "Roone had this genius for understanding what felt good to viewers. And Cokie felt good. She just brought an ease and confidence and comfortableness. One of the things Roone understood was that television has you in strangers' living rooms. So you better not make them uneasy. And Cokie was a good guest in a stranger's living room."

Then in midlife she became a storyteller, publishing her first book at age fifty-four: *We Are Our Mothers' Daughters*, which reached number one on the *New York Times* bestseller list. Four other bestsellers followed (five if you include a children's version of one history book), all of which focused on researching and resurrecting the contributions women have always made to American history, while seldom getting the recognition they deserve. As Catherine Allgor, head of the Massachusetts Historical Society, told me, "The biggest thing that she did was let Americans know there was a history out there they weren't aware of. That just made a huge difference."

There's one story that sums up what those books were all about. In *Founding Mothers*, which focuses on the Revolutionary period, Cokie writes about the enormous contribution Martha Washington made to the American cause, spending winters in camp with the soldiers and bolstering their spirits. And it really bothered her that the sign outside of Mt. Vernon, down the Potomac River from the capital, read HOME OF GEORGE WASHINGTON, with no mention of Martha. As Mary Thompson, a historian at Mt. Vernon, tells the tale, Cokie relentlessly pestered the director of the site to change the sign. Thompson usually drove into the grounds on a back road but one day happened to pass through the front gate, and saw that the sign had been altered to read, HOME OF GEORGE AND MARTHA WASHINGTON. Her reaction was to shout, "Yay, Cokie!" because "I'm sure that was her doing."

"Politics is our family business," Cokie once told *People* magazine, and if anything, that was an understatement. Her first ancestor to serve in Congress was W. C. C. Claiborne, elected to the House from Tennessee in 1797 at the age of twenty-three— the youngest federal lawmaker in the country's entire history. So her parents were part of a long and well-established tradition. Author Steve Hess counted eleven Claibornes (Cokie's middle name and her mother's maiden name) in major public office over seven generations and rated her family as the second most prominent in American political history, outranking the Kennedys and trailing only the Roosevelts, because they had two presidents. She really became a journalist by accident, mainly because she married one. When a *Washington Post* reporter asked her, "Did you consider entering politics yourself?" she gave this revealing answer: "Well, I certainly admire people who do it. But Steve and I met when we were 18 and 19. He was always going to be a journalist from the time he was, like, 9 or 10 years old. So, it would have been very hard on him if I had gone into politics. I have always felt semi-guilty about it. But I've sort of assuaged my guilt by writing about it and feeling like I'm educating people about the government and how to be good voters and good citizens. And that's been true through my reporting, but also through writing these history books. I feel like letting people know what this country is all about and how it all happened is not *not* public service. [Laughs.]"

Reporting the news and writing history, however, didn't fully erase her guilt. She wanted more latitude to espouse the causes she felt deeply about, and in 2002, at age fifty-eight, she quit her full-time job as coanchor of ABC's Sunday show *This Week*. While she had many reasons for doing that, one of the most important was freeing her up to spend more time and energy directly promoting the welfare of women and children. She was diagnosed with breast cancer that same year, and while she had decided to leave the show before she got sick, her illness reinforced her decision to reorder her priorities. After a lot of research, she joined the board of Save the Children, the worldwide relief organization, and Charlie MacCormack, then the organization's CEO, recalls meeting Cokie for the first time: "She talked about her commitment to girls and women, it was pretty central to what she hoped would be her legacy. It was clear that was really consuming to her, a passion, and that's what we needed." I asked if she talked about her diagnosis, and MacCormack, whose wife also had breast cancer, replied, "Oh yes. She said 'I've got to rebalance my time, because I don't know how much time I have left.'"

"Passion" is the right word to describe Cokie's work as an advocate, and her value system was completely clear. Carolyn Miles, who succeeded MacCormack as head of Save the Children, described those values: "She was always standing up for women and mothers. And I think she felt as a mother herself, that moms were the key. Not that she didn't care about fathers. Of course she did. But I saw time after time that she was always pushing to enable mothers to have some knowledge and some capability to change the direction of their kids' lives. She really believed very deeply in that."

So yes, through her visibility and celebrity, Cokie was an inspiration and a role model for innumerable women and girls. She was portrayed on *Saturday Night Live*, mentioned on *The West Wing*, pictured in comic strips like *Doonesbury*, and featured on magazine covers. She joked with Jay Leno, sang with Garrison Keillor, sparred with Conan O'Brien, balanced a pencil on her nose for David Letterman, and was the answer to numerous crossword puzzle clues. Many dogs, and at least one dairy cow, were named for her. In 1990, *Spy* magazine ran a drawing documenting all her connections and associations and headlined it, "Cokie Roberts—Moderately Well-Known Broadcast Journalist or Center of the Universe?" They were only half joking.

But as I think about her legacy, I'm convinced that her private life was as significant as her public life. Few of us can be a TV star or bestselling author. Every one of us can be a good person. Everyone can learn a lot from how she treated others. Cokie did something for someone else virtually every day of her life, especially people who were not famous or wealthy or influential. I tried to capture that spirit in my eulogy: "During the last days of her life she was hospitalized at NIH, and when I would pull up the valet parkers, all immigrants and not very fluent in English, would say to me, 'We're praying for Miss Cokie.' She became very friendly with one of her nurses, Letitia, and absolutely insisted that I rummage through her recipe box at home and find a recipe for crawfish corn bread she wanted Letitia to have. The author of that recipe, by the way, a man named Big Lou, is serving a life sentence in Louisiana's Angola prison, but he was Cokie's friend too. And then there was Judith, another nurse, who had two small children at home and was pregnant with a third. Cokie kept bugging her, 'Judith I want to see pictures of those children,' and last Saturday, in the last hours of the last day that Cokie was conscious, Judith finally relented and showed Cokie pictures on her phone. Cokie's face just lit up with that incandescent smile we all have loved for so long. 'Judith,' she exclaimed, 'what beautiful children!' and the two embraced. That moment captured the Cokie I'll remember most. Caring about someone else, helping them feel good about themselves, opening her heart and her arms and making the world around her a better brighter place."

Through our long life together, we agreed that people learn best through stories, not sermons, through experience, not ideology. I've collected a lot of Cokie stories over the years, and I tell a lot of them here. But I also know what I don't know. There were important parts of her life that I did not share, starting with her female friendships. I was not there when she kept vigil outside a hospital room after a friend's cancer surgery, or when she flew to Massachusetts to attend the funeral of a friend's son, or when she counseled and consoled dozens of young colleagues about how to handle brutal bosses or benighted boyfriends. And I did not want to be the guy who tried to explain or interpret those friendships. I wanted her friends to speak for themselves, and when they do so in these pages, many of them make the same point. Cokie was their moral touchstone, their guide to good behavior. As her childhood friend and college roommate Cinda Pratt Perlman told me, "Early on, I remember thinking, this is what I'm going to do. Instead of wearing one of those little bracelets that says, 'WWJD, What Would Jesus Do?,' I'd have one made saying 'WWCD, What Would Cokie Do?' Now we're talking. That's the real deal."

That's why her friend Bob Murphy recalls sitting in the cathedral at her funeral and realizing that every person there thought they had a "special relationship" with her and "were best friends." Then he asked himself, "How does one person have the energy, the time, the bandwidth to have several thousand best friends?" It's a good question, with a complex answer. Some of those friends were men, of course. Cokie attended three different

funerals for Bob's relatives—for both of his parents and his partner Pete—and he recalls, "To have Cokie feel and see and honor
my relationship with Pete, that was a gift beyond anything I ever
expected to happen."

She deeply loved her male relatives: her father, Hale; her two
brothers (Tommy became one of Washington's most prominent
lawyer-lobbyists; Billy died in infancy); her son, Lee; four grand-
sons, numerous uncles, cousins, nephews, spouses, and in-laws.
She liked to say that the two of us stayed "crazy nuts" about each
other for more than half a century, and in *We Are Our Mothers'
Daughters* she wrote, "This book is about women. But it would
not be possible without a man. To my husband Steven—my mentor, my fan, my lover, my muse—this book is dedicated." After
Cokie died, many of my former students told me a similar story:
they always noticed that when I talked about her, my whole man-
ner changed. My tone, apparently, grew softer and sweeter. And
they sat there thinking, I want a partner who talks that way about
me after so many years together.

But there's also a bright line, a clear arc, that runs through
many of the stories in this book—Cokie's commitment to celebrating and supporting, praising and promoting, other women.
Those two words she had added to the sign at Mt. Vernon, "and
Martha," embodied that commitment. Through every part of her
life, in public and in private, her sense of sisterhood was prominent and powerful. "I think Cokie believed, maybe, women
would be the ones to save the planet," said Diane Sawyer. She
was a true feminist, but she didn't become one by reading books

or spouting theories. Her feminism flowed from her life experience, from the obstacles she faced, the models she followed, and the faith she embraced. And I've identified at least five themes, or influences, that helped shape the person Cokie became.

Start with discrimination. Her first job after college was working for a small TV production company, and within a year, she was hosting her own weekly talk show on NBC's Washington affiliate. It was a measure of life in the mid-'60s that when we got married, we didn't even discuss whose job was more important. I was working on the city staff of the *New York Times*, and we both simply assumed that she'd quit and join me in New York. When she did, however, doors were slammed in her face. This woman, who eventually authored six bestsellers, was told repeatedly, at publications like *Newsweek*, that they simply did not hire women as writers. "One other thing," she said years later in the *New York Times*. "While these men were saying we couldn't have the jobs, their hands were on our knees." In our book about our marriage, *From This Day Forward*, Cokie connected those encounters to her own blossoming rebellion: "The experiences that many of us were having—being turned down for jobs because we were women—seemed to be happening to each of us individually. We'd make bitter jokes about a prospective boss asking how many words we typed, something they never asked our male counterparts, but as far as we were concerned, that's just the way things were. It was only after we all started talking to each other that we realized we were being illegally discriminated against and that's when the modern feminist movement came into flower. But the period where each of us was alone in our misery was a very difficult period."

The second influence was her faith. She was a devout Roman Catholic who attended Mass regularly and lived by the teachings of her church. I'm Jewish, and the religious difference was a huge hurdle for us to overcome, but I came to understand a basic truth: it was her religious foundation that produced many of the traits I loved so dearly about her. As a small child she was taught that every person was created "in the image and likeness of God" and she treated people that way. Her friend Cinda Perlman recalls a night when Cokie was twelve or thirteen, and the two girls found a book called *The Way of Divine Love* written by Sister Josefa Menéndez, a Spanish nun who belonged to the Sacred Heart order, the same order that ran Stone Ridge, the school they attended. They stayed up all night, reading passages to each other, and Cinda remembers it as a "very transforming experience." Cokie, she says, "never forgot the sense that her life was meant to be used in some way, that it was a God-given gift and she needed to make it the very best she could. That's what she owed this Creator."

Nuns like Sister Josefa were strongly connected to the third influence that molded Cokie: her education. She always attended all-female schools, first at Stone Ridge and then at Wellesley, and in both places, she once noted, girls talked all the time because "there's nobody else *to* talk." All of her models of authority and inspiration were women, and she felt so strongly about their contribution that she dedicated her book *Founding Mothers* "to my own Founding Mothers." In particular she honored "the religious of the Society of the Sacred Heart, the RSCJ's, who take girls seriously—a radical notion in the 1950s." She remained loyal to that order and to Stone Ridge her whole life, serving on the board, singing in the choir at Christmas Eve Mass, and making a video, not long before she died, urging donors to contribute to the school's capital campaign. A new theater on the campus is named for her.

Wellesley left its mark too, even though some of the professors were actually men, and there were no nuns around. In fact, Wellesley was the first—and only—school any of the three Boggs children attended at any level that was not Catholic. There's a favorite family story that after her parents dropped Cokie off in September of 1960 Lindy turned to Hale, burst into tears, and complained, "I've left my baby at a Yankee, Protestant Republican school." Cokie's main activity in college, besides politics, was singing with an a cappella group called the Wellesley Widows, and she always enjoyed the way women's voices could harmonize with each other, in song and in story. Lynn Sherr, an ABC correspondent who was a year ahead of Cokie in college, feels that the Wellesley experience taught a lesson of self-confidence and self-reliance: "Don't let them define who you are. You know who you are and what you can do." It also created a bond of sisterhood, and Sherr recalls the first election night when both of them were part of the network's coverage: "She came over to me on the set and said, 'Isn't it great having two girls on the set?' And it really was supportive and wonderful."

Cokie chose the title of her first book aptly—and deliberately. She was her own mother's daughter in many ways, as she described in this interview with *People* magazine: "Mama gave us the role model of someone who knew how to juggle. She was always there, and yet she was always working. We thought she was the most beautiful woman alive. I was shocked to discover that other people didn't think their mothers were beautiful. When we got bigger, the most striking thing was that she was the most reliable woman around. My friends and I would be in school until 10 at night putting out the school paper, and it was Mama who would come and get us even though she had worked all day." *Lear's* once referred to "The Myth of the Boggs Women," a myth that roughly translates into, "Do Everything You Can for Everybody Else All of the Time."

That title, "the most reliable woman around," is certainly one Cokie could have proudly claimed. But her mother's influence went far beyond cosmetics and carpools. She refers twice to her mother "working," but in fact what Lindy did during Cokie's childhood was very traditional for a woman of her age and place: supporting and advising her husband's political career while volunteering to run, along with other congressional wives and local Black women, many of Washington's social service organizations. Cokie's determination to write women's history, to add "and Martha" to the nation's chronicle, came directly from her mother's experience, and the other extraordinary women Lindy worked with in those early years. "Growing up in Washington in the 1940s and 1950s, I saw the influence of women like my mother, and then the women that she associated with: Mrs. Lyndon Johnson, Mrs. Albert Gore, and Mrs. Gerald Ford," she told one interviewer. "They were very influential in the community of Washington itself, and extremely influential in their husbands' campaigns and careers."

Then tragedy altered the direction of Lindy's life. In 1972, Cokie's father was killed in a plane crash while campaigning for a fellow congressman in Alaska. A few months later her mother won his seat in a special election and held it for the next eighteen years. Lindy had moved from backstage to center stage, from being "and Lindy" to wielding power in her own right. And when Cokie and I returned to Washington in 1977, she had a new role model: a mother who had already authored landmark legislation guaranteeing equal credit for women, and become the first woman to chair a national party convention. So when Cokie started covering Congress for NPR, her mother was a member, not a wife, a lawmaker, not an advice giver. "When my son was small," she told *People*, "I'd pull Mama off the House floor and cry that it was 9 in the evening and I wasn't home with my child. Mama would look at me and say, 'He's fine.' The mothers of many of the women of my generation were the great guilt inculcators; my mother was the great guilt remover." When she contributed an essay to the book *The Lives Our Mothers Leave Us*, Cokie said simply: "When I'm being my very best self, I am being my mother's daughter."

The fifth influence on Cokie was continuity, a deeply felt understanding of the essential roles that women have always played—mothering, nurturing, caretaking. Instead of rebelling against those customs, she embraced them. No one fought harder for women's rights, yet no one believed more strongly in women's historic mission. She was a conservative and a radical all at once, battling for a better future while cherishing the virtues of the past. And she wore her devotion to tradition proudly. She was old-fashioned and wanted people to know it. "I know exactly who I am, and I am comfortable with that," she told a reporter from the Associated Press. "I'm just sort of a normal person who knows a lot about a few things and a little about a lot of things and I'm not shy about talking about it." Marc Burstein, a longtime ABC producer, remembers the first Sunday morning that Cokie appeared on the network show then hosted by David Brinkley: "It was probably the first time I met her and she said, 'There's three things you need to know about me. I'm married to the same man for 20 years. I live in the house I grew up in and I go to church every Sunday.' And with that she let out that famous Cokie laugh and she said, 'If you remember those three things about me, we're going to get along just great.' And I never forgot those three things. The only thing that changed was the number of years you were married."

In her introduction to *We Are Our Mothers' Daughters*, Cokie expressed her fervent faith in her sisters and their common enterprise: "I'm always struck by the similarities in women's stories, no matter how different they may superficially seem. That's because of the thread of continuity with women throughout the ages, that sense that we are doing what women have always done even as we pioneer across cultural divides or declare a revolution." She described a small museum we used to visit in Greece, not far from the battlefield in ancient Marathon, and then added: "Here was nothing of heroic dimensions, nothing on a grand scale: in one case, needles, buttons; in another, jewelry, pots for makeup; in another, frying pans and toys. Here objects from the everyday lives of women from thousands of years ago overwhelmed me with their familiarity. I could have opened the cases, put on their jewels, and taken up their tools, and picked up where they left off without a moment's hesitation or confusion. What was left from the lives of the men? Objects of war and objects of worship, recognizable for soldiers and priests, but what of the others? That little museum has always symbolized for me the great strength of women. We are connected throughout time and regardless of place." On the back of her tombstone in Congressional Cemetery is carved this admonition to other women: "Put on the jewels and take up the tools."

Our friend Max Byrd, a teacher and novelist, had a mentor when we were at Harvard named Walter Jackson Bate, an expert on the British writer Samuel Johnson. Johnson, Bate would say, "became the man he was supposed to be." The same could be said of Cokie, Max said: "She became the woman she was supposed to be." And that's what I hope comes through in this book. Cokie had a brilliant idea in organizing *We Are Our Mothers' Daughters*. Each chapter is based on a different role that women play. Some are personal—wife, sister—and some are public—soldier, politician. I have borrowed—okay, stolen—the same organizing principle. There are chapters here devoted to her public role as a journalist, author, and advocate, and others to her private role as wife and mother, friend and believer. Through them all I have a very simple goal. To tell stories. Some will make you cheer or laugh or cry. And some, I hope, will inspire you to be more like Cokie, to be a good person, to lead a good life.

Wife

"I feel pretty, I feel pretty."

We met in the summer of 1962, between our sophomore and junior years of college, at a student political meeting on the campus of Ohio State. Cokie was eighteen at the time, I was nineteen, and this is her version: "I saw Steven across the yard and he looked familiar to me because I knew his twin brother.

And I kept thinking, 'Is that Marc Roberts? He doesn't quite look like Marc Roberts, but he looks a whole lot like Marc Roberts.' And then I got up close to him and he had a name tag, so I said, 'Are you Marc Roberts' brother?' And he said, 'Yes, are you Barbara Boggs' sister?' And that's how we met."

I am convinced she was wearing a pair of charcoal-gray Bermuda shorts at the time. She insisted she never owned such a garment, and spent the next fifty-seven years correcting me on this point—and countless others. Still, the attraction was immediate. We started flirting and passing notes to each other during endless debates over long-forgotten issues, and Cokie, who saved everything, somehow preserved them. "You're so efficient it hurts," I wrote, and she replied: "I'm the youngest child of an insane family—somebody has to be efficient, otherwise we'd starve!" I answered, "Be efficient, but Jeezus—don't ever get comfortable, it's such a deadly disease." That shows how ignorant I was about myself. Comfort was exactly what I was looking for, and little did I know that this beautiful girl with an adorable upturned nose and brilliant blue eyes was going to provide it for more than half a century. But she was looking for the same thing. Her final word about comfort as a deadly disease: "Would that I could ever have the opportunity to catch it."

I knew from the beginning that I had met a very special person— smart and sweet, sexy and sassy all at once. She gave a speech during one of the conference sessions, and, as she recalled many years later in the *New York Times*, "that impressed him because it was highly unusual for women to speak." It was also highly unusual in 1962 for women to think about a career, and Cokie was a creature of her time. "My goal in life was marriage, then mother-hood," she wrote. "I wanted to get married as soon as possible after college, do something interesting for a while, but have ba-bies as fast as I could. Then I thought I would stay home, do good things in the community, and enhance my husband's career. That's what suburban life in the 1950s seemed to dictate."

We returned that fall to school in Boston, where my dorm at Harvard and hers at Wellesley were only a few miles apart. But I was slow to call, so she took the initiative, inviting me to the ju-nior show, where she had a singing part. After the show we went to the local Howard Johnson's for something to eat. I still remem-ber the green dress she was wearing, and her friend Cinda—who understood that in the early '60s, our religious differences posed a huge barrier to our relationship—remembers the scene when she returned to the dorm: "She's singing 'I feel pretty, I feel pretty,' she did that whole song from West Side Story and I thought, Oh my God, this man makes her very happy, makes her feel special. And I found it hard to watch, thinking that it was going to end badly, put it that way. But it was really fun to watch her be so in love."

Then I stopped calling—again. I was a typical guy, petrified of commitment, but many of my friends visited Wellesley regularly and they'd bring back greetings—"Cokie Boggs says hi." Then in March we both were going to Washington for a conference on a domestic version of the Peace Corps run by Cokie's sister. Someone organized a group to drive down together, and I vividly recall approaching the car parked on a side street in Cambridge. Cokie was sitting in the back seat, and when I saw her through the window I said to myself, "You idiot, this is the girl . . ." Or words to that effect. A bunch of guys were supposed to stay at Cokie's house for the weekend, but the others all dropped out, leaving me as the only houseguest.

That night I was ensconced in Cokie's girlhood room (later our daughter's room), and because I had been spending the winter in New England I had a lousy cough. I've told the story many times of what happened next: I heard a knock on the door, and because this was 1963, I figured it wasn't Cokie. Instead, in wafted Lindy—my future mother-in-law, the future member of Congress and ambassador to the Vatican—wearing a peach-colored negligee and bearing a glass of some magical potion. "Why, darlin'," she said, "you sound terrible, drink this." I was in shock. I had never met anybody remotely like this back home in Bayonne, NJ. So dutifully I downed the glass, which I assume was heavily laced with bourbon. The joke in the family is that I fell in love with Lindy first and eventually got around to Cokie, and there's some truth to that. The next night, after the conference, Cokie and I sat up talking far into the early morning. We discussed the religious difference that frightened Cinda about our future and started to see—timidly, tentatively—a possible path forward for us. At some point she scrambled us some eggs for breakfast and we got in the car to drive back to Boston. "We smooched all the way back even though there were other people in the car—but that part was embarrassing," she later recalled.

Many tears and troubles lay ahead, but after that weekend we never parted. A few weeks later, during spring break, we had a date in New York, where Cokie was staying at a friend's apartment. Her memory: "We went for a walk through Central Park, then to a movie, then to the Russian Tea Room. We had apricots and plums and Steve said he liked those colors together, and from there on out I kept desperately trying to find apricot-and-plum combinations." Again we stayed up all night, and when dawn broke, she headed for church and I took the bus home to New Jersey. A few days later I wrote to her: "We've been found out already, my dear. I trundled into the house at 6:45 to find my grandfather already up, making breakfast." When I awoke in midafternoon, "you should have seen my mother's face when I told her the reason we stayed up is that you had to go to 6 o'clock Mass anyway." I ended by saying, "I remember with a smile something you said at about 4:30 a.m. Sunday morning. I asked if you were tired and you said, 'No, I want to stay up and play with you.' Well, I'm not very tired, and I can think of nothing that I would rather do than stay up and play with you. But you are not here (funny thing) and I will have to be content with my dreams of you." Cokie wrote many years later: "We still told each other it was just a spring romance. And I certainly thought that was the safest thing to say. Anything more would have scared him off. But we were very happy and clearly in love."

Yes, we were. That's why our wedding rings are inscribed, FOREVER SPRING. When I was with her, I felt excited and elated but also comfortable and confident. I had never really had a serious girlfriend before, and with Cokie my anxieties melted away. Whatever we did or wherever we went, it would be okay. One night I brought her to the *Crimson*, the school newspaper where I spent a great deal of time. One of my closest pals, Joe Russin, describes his reaction to meeting her: "I remember turning around and seeing Cokie and thought, holy moly, that is the most beautiful woman I've ever seen. Cokie just had this effect on people. When she walked into a room, the room changed. There was a whole new focus. She was the center of attention. She was the one people wanted to talk to. She was the one who just captured your eye." She captured your mind, not just your eye, and when she came to meals at my Harvard residence hall, Eliot House, she always held her own with the self-important— and somewhat startled—males at the table. Inspired by those encounters, I wrote an article for the *Crimson* saying women should play a bigger role in the college's intellectual life, and I received a call from the president of Radcliffe, then the women's arm of Harvard. "Could you speak at Radcliffe?" she asked. "I've never met a Harvard man with your views." Cokie came to the event, cheering me on and symbolizing what I was only beginning to realize. She was already shaping and shifting my sense of the world.

Still, our religions, and my reluctance, kept clouding our happiness. At some point that spring Cokie wrote me a letter that tried to explain her emotions. What has survived is a draft, written in pencil on a piece of paper ripped from a spiral notebook. Apparently, we'd had yet another painful conversation the night before and she wrote, "Last night, for the second time at Wellesley, I cried. The only other time was out of sheer physical agony, so it doesn't really count." My inattentiveness, as usual, was cause for complaint. "So many different emotions are running around in me and I don't know what to do with any of them," she wrote. "A good deal of the reason that I was upset about your not calling me was that I was upset at myself for being upset. I think you know that I too have wanted to leave our relationship undefined, to myself as well as to you. So it frightens me when I see these evidences of caring so much, perhaps because it means I'm forcing an issue." She understood that the "problem of my Catholicism and your Judaism . . . would be insoluble." Yet she added: "More than anything I want to keep seeing you. I don't want to give up these happy times, and I don't want to lend them an air of tragedy."

And that's what happened. No matter how great the stress, or how high the obstacles, we wanted to keep seeing each other. But we were apart for the summer—she went home to Washington; I stayed in Cambridge—and it took a while for our romance to rekindle that fall. She wrote to me at one point—again, all I have is a draft composed on notebook paper—expressing her feelings: "Last spring when you told me that you thought you were falling in love with me 'in a happy kind of way,' I was upset, because I knew that would mean that we would have to discuss our whole relationship. I didn't want to do that. I wanted to keep on existing in the happy, or 'happified,' unreal state I had been living in. When you told me you loved me, or thought you did, much of that changed. Until that time I would not admit to myself that I could be in love with you. Once the issue had been forced, however, I felt nothing but happiness at the realization that I loved you." The previous spring, she admits, she had left school determined to "do" something about our relationship. "Right now," she concludes, "I am not. Maybe I am being unrealistic but that is a common feeling of young girls in love. Remember that, and treat me gently . . ."

I wish I could say that I did treat her gently, but I didn't always do that. I was still very young, still very confused about being in love at all, let alone with a Catholic, and writing an honors thesis that took a great deal of time and effort. "He would call me on Saturday morning and break a date for that night, saying he had to work too hard," Cokie recalled. "So I finally caught on and started going to Cambridge early on Saturday morning and studying in the stacks of the Harvard library so he couldn't reach me to break the date. I would just show up at the appointed hour."

We didn't know it at the time of course, but those Saturdays foreshadowed a pattern that marked much of our life together. I was the campus correspondent for the *New York Times* and often had an assignment to cover a sporting event, a track meet or a lacrosse game, and she would come with me. The *Times* paid the princely sum of $5 for my work, but there was a restaurant in Harvard Square called Cronin's that had a dinner special, three courses for $1.98, so my paltry payment covered dinner for two! Many evenings Cokie would sing somewhere in Boston with the Widows, and I became a groupie. Cokie, of course, was the president of the group and the emcee of their performances, so I learned the words to all their songs and the punch lines to all her jokes. Good training for marriage.

As graduation approached, we were both getting the same advice: stop seeing each other. Her friend Cinda Perlman remembers weighing in: "The more she told me about you, the more I thought, uh-oh, I can see where this is heading. This may be a disaster in the making. She's going to fall head over heels, she already has. And it can't possibly go anywhere. And she's going to be heartbroken. And I can't bear to think of that. So I gave her my very sage advice. I said, Cokie, I think you've got to break it off sooner than later because it's just going to be so sad when he says, there's no way I can marry you."

During this period I received a five-page single-spaced letter from my father, pressing the same case. We shared a deep relationship, he was my first editor and biggest cheerleader, so his words wounded me deeply: "I could never understand a person who prizes integrity being married in the name of a religion in which he does not believe and in which he has not been raised. Nor can I understand a girl who professes to prize integrity asking a man to do so." He concluded: "I can tell you positively that the longer you go on, the more severe will be the trauma and the deeper the heartbreak. For I can see no viable solution, nor have you suggested any to me." My reply spoke for myself, but I believe it reflected what Cokie would have told Cinda and other skeptics at the time. "Throughout the letter," I wrote to Dad, "you showed marked insensitivity to one great factor in this matter:

my love for Cokie." And I added: "I hope that I can continue to love, and still preserve my faith in our ideals. I continue to hope because I love; you see no hope, but you do not love." I have to say that things changed dramatically over the next few years. Dad did come to love Cokie, in large part because she made such a concerted effort to understand his concerns and ease his fears. Eventually she became known as "the best Jew in the family," and my father finally conceded, "It would be so much easier to oppose this match if it wasn't so obvious she's the perfect girl for you." (Our mothers eventually became devoted friends as well. Toward the end of their lives, both had moved to Washington, and they would come to Sunday dinner, hold hands, and admire their mutual great-grandchildren.)

But that reconciliation was still in the future. After graduation, Cokie and I both moved to Washington. She took up residence in her old bedroom and started work for a small TV production company. I lived in a series of group houses downtown and became the research assistant for the bureau chief of the *New York Times*, James "Scotty" Reston. The painful conversations Cokie had had back at Wellesley with her roommates continued with Jean Firstenberg, her coworker at the production company who became a lifelong friend. As they shared a cocktail after work, Jean recalled, "All we would talk about was how could she get you to marry her. She knew what she wanted. What she wanted was a life with you, that that was her goal and she wasn't going to be deterred."

My goals were not so clear. I was still wrestling with torn

loyalties—to my family and to Cokie—and she recalls, "They were agonizing years, they really were. I was traveling a lot, producing TV shows in different cities, and I remember miserable phone conversations late at night in hotel rooms." There was another miserable conversation that Cokie recalled vividly: "I decided I was wasting the best years of my life. I was twenty-two and I was about to be an old maid! Steven began to get a sense of how fed up I was one day when we stopped at a rest stop on the Jersey Turnpike and decided to share a Danish pastry. I was raised to believe a woman always gave a man the best piece of everything, and Steven was raised to expect that. That day, when I ate the center out of the Danish and left him the crust, he knew I was truly ticked."

Truly ticked but deeply devoted. During her travels for work she found herself in Cincinnati over Rosh Hashanah. "One of the oldest temples in Reform Judaism, the Plum Street Temple, is there," she recalled. "I had no idea that tickets were required for services, so I went up to the door and the usher asked, 'What do you want?' I said, 'I want to come in, I want to go to services.' The guy said okay and he walked me down the aisle and said in this huge stage whisper so the entire congregation could hear, 'Here's one that came without her boyfriend.' It was not a good moment."

Actually it was, because it demonstrated how hard we were trying to figure this religion thing out, and one way to do that was learn more about each other's traditions. We were coming to realize that our differences were not "insoluble" as she had once written, and so many others believed. We both were old-fashioned, we both were intensely loyal to our tribes and traditions, and we admired and respected that in each other. In all our years together one word that was never spoken was "conversion," because we knew that was not possible for either one of us. What was possible was the growing understanding that we shared values if not theologies. We wanted to live the same way and raise our kids the same way. What we agreed on was far deeper and more important than our disagreements. My dad was wrong, and I was right. As that old rock song put it, "Love will find a way."

But still, I wouldn't pull the trigger or pop the question. In January of 1966, she wrote me a long letter on NBC stationery that started, "Perhaps we are finally growing up." Apparently, we'd had a difficult talk the night before that had not, for once, ended in tears. "I've always told you that it's easy for me to imagine being married to you," she wrote, but it was the wedding that worried her. All the tensions between us and our families would crystallize around the ceremony, she feared: "I see them as horrible, painful things that will be suffered through in order that we might be happy. That's one of the reasons why I keep wanting to squeeze some decision out of you. . . . Once we decide when we want to get married it's going to take months of cajoling, crying and gruesome conversations before the actual event."

What finally squeezed me into action, however, was her ultimatum. Cokie recalled: "I finally said, 'I'm not doing this anymore, I'm going to California.' And I really meant it." I knew it was the right girl and the wrong time. I was only twenty-three and just starting my career in journalism, but she had none of those doubts: "I said this is the only time. If you want this girl *this* is the time." And I did want this girl, deeply and desperately. We decided to take a carriage ride through Central Park as the right romantic setting for the formal proposal, but the words stuck in my throat. We were almost at the end of the ride when I finally stammered out, "Will you marry me?" The joke in the family is that I actually proposed by saying, "Oh, all right, Cokie." I've said to my students countless times that who you marry is the most important decision you ever make, nothing else is even close. Many of them say it's the best advice I've ever given them, and fortunately, when I was faced with that decision in my own life, I got it right. Exactly right.

But the "gruesome conversations" Cokie anticipated still had to be endured. She insisted that we fly to Washington so I could formally ask her father for his permission. And first, I had to call my parents to tell them what we were doing. True to form, I waited until the last possible moment, and the plane was boarding by the time I called home. My mother answered, and I blurted into the phone, "I'm going to Washington and Cokie and I are getting engaged." Mom burst into tears, and I hung up the phone, yet another profile in courage. Things went a bit better with her family. Her parents had many close friends back in New Orleans who were Jewish, and Cokie's sister Barbara had been engaged to a Jewish man. The relationship did not last, but her parents had come to terms with the idea of a Jewish son-in-law. So having a child marry outside their faith was a lot easier for them to accept than it was for my parents, who grew up in an insular community and had few non-Jewish acquaintances. Still, I was nervous. After all, my future father-in-law was the Democratic whip of the House at the time and a close friend of President Johnson. He was nervous too, however, and had retreated to his tomato patch in the front yard. Cokie pushed me out the door and I approached cautiously. Cokie and I knew we'd face some problems, I told him, but we were confident we could overcome them. "Yes, I do think you'll have problems," he replied, "but not half as many problems as I'll have if I try to tell Cokie who to marry."

He was right about that. Cokie was only twenty-two, but "she knew what she wanted," and she was determined to make it happen. That spring we got an unexpected assist from Rome. I had balked at a rule that said that if an interfaith couple wanted to be married in a Catholic ceremony, both partners had to sign a promise to raise their children in the church. I was ready to promise Cokie anything but didn't want outsiders dictating our decisions. Then Pope Paul VI changed the rule so that only the Catholic partner had to take the pledge, and Cokie was ecstatic. She called her friend Marcia Burick and exclaimed, "Hail to the Pope!" And she teased me that the Holy Father had removed my last excuse.

Our wedding plans symbolized the spirit of inclusion we hoped would mark our life together. The ceremony would be at home, not in a church. There would be a priest but also a rabbi. And we'd get married under a chuppah, a traditional Jewish wedding canopy. One problem: we couldn't find a rabbi to participate.

Cokie tried hard but struck out, even calling a White House aide, rumor had it, who was an ordained clergyman. When she told him what she wanted he whispered, "I'll call you back from a pay phone." But even he wouldn't come, and the whole search was both demeaning and depressing. Finally my mother came up with a brilliant solution. In Jewish tradition, she pointed out, a rabbi is an elder of the tribe, not a priest in the Christian sense. So why not ask a Jewish elder to participate, like, say, Arthur Goldberg? Goldberg, a good friend of Cokie's parents, had just left the Supreme Court to become the American ambassador to the United Nations. He agreed to come, and gave a lovely talk about Jewish teachings on marriage, which included the biblical admonition, "Do not cause a woman to weep because God counts her tears." I'm afraid I didn't always follow his advice in the years to come, but his presence meant that my parents and their friends felt recognized and respected.

Once the day was set Lindy asked Hale who he wanted to invite among his fellow congressmen. In a fit of irritation, he growled, "All the Democrats." Now this was after the Democratic landslide of 1964, there were more than three hundred Democrats in the House, and most of them came. So did assorted cabinet officers and Supreme Court justices and President and Mrs. Johnson—1,500 guests in all. My in-laws couldn't afford a caterer for that many, so Lindy cooked herself, while farming out assignments to dozens of friends. For days before the wedding you'd come into the kitchen and see a sign on the oven saying, I'M A HAM, TAKE ME OUT AT FOUR. One of Cokie's favorite stories about her mother came from this period. "I walked into the kitchen after work one day," she wrote, "and there at the stove stood my mother, a baby on her hip, a spoon in her hand, and the phone crooked into her neck. In one large swaying motion she soothed the baby, stirred the pot full of pickles, and dictated a speech into the telephone." Then she added: "A hard act to follow? No kidding."

On the day of the wedding, Cokie's grandmother Coco wouldn't let her into the bathroom they shared to get ready. "I stood in the hallway outside the door, begging, 'Coco, I really need to get in there, I'm getting married,'" the bride remembered. "And she kept saying, 'Darling, just another minute, just another minute. If you give me a whole minute, I'll let you borrow my eye shadow.' When I finally did get in the bathroom, my father started banging on the door, shouting, 'Cokie, you've got to come out of there. The president's here.' And I blew up: 'Well, the bride's not!'" When she finally did emerge, and the music had started, the ring bearer, our five-year-old nephew Hale, announced that he had lost one of the rings. Cokie had another fit, saying she could not get married without the right ring: "No, I'm not going to do it. Daddy, the symbolism of this is just all wrong." After all of our strenuous attempts at inclusion—from the location and the celebrants to the Jewish chuppah—her father was on the brink of exasperation. "Cokie," he shot back, "don't you think there's enough symbolism going on here for one night?"

We had been apartment hunting over the summer, and I found a two-bedroom rent-controlled bargain for $185 a month on

West Seventy-Fifth Street, one subway stop from my office near Times Square. An airline strike prevented Cokie from getting to New York to see it, so I had to sign the lease myself. The previous tenants wanted us to pay them a thousand dollars for a fake marble floor they'd installed in the hallway, but we didn't have that kind of money, and out of spite they ripped up the floor before they left. So when Cokie first saw the apartment, weeks before the wedding, she was greeted by bare concrete—and burst into tears. After the honeymoon, when we returned to our little love nest, a sign in the elevator said, NO HEAT OR HOT WATER UNTIL FURTHER NOTICE. Welcome to New York!

As I've said, we didn't even have a conversation about whose job was more important. So although Cokie was already hosting her own TV show, we both assumed my career took precedence. (That would happen many more times over the next eleven years.) It was a hard adjustment for her, far harder than I understood at the time. No matter how much she wanted to get married, the isolation and idleness suffocated her spirit. She often told this story to illustrate her turmoil: "In the end it was good for us—for me—to leave Washington. But it was very hard to pick up and become another person and not have any separate identity from Steven at all. I would go job hunting and get rejected and become depressed about it. The days grew very long. It reached the point where I would say to myself, 'You must do X today,' so that I'd leave the house in an effort to cheer myself up. I'd scold myself saying things like, 'You must go to the bank by three o'clock in the afternoon.' One day after Christmas I set a goal of returning a wedding present to Georg Jensen, a fancy New York store. But in my depressed state, I couldn't quite manage to get dressed. I decided that was all right, I could do this without getting dressed. I put on a blue coat and a hat that matched it and went to the store in my nightgown! I figured it was terribly important to fulfill my pathetic goal for the day, and if I had waited and tried to get dressed, I was likely to fail.

"When I arrived at Jensen's return counter, standing right there was the person who gave me the wedding present. There are eight million people in the city of New York and the friend who gave me the present shows up at the same time I do at the return counter. What are the odds of that happening? I was so flustered that when the salesclerk asked 'Should I put this on your account?' I mumbled, 'Yes, yes, yes,' and gave her my name. I didn't have an account, I was just trying to get out of there, but I couldn't move fast enough. I was caught in the act. Fortunately the friend thought it was funny and as a gesture of forgiveness asked me to come along with him to Nelson Rockefeller's swearing-in as governor. Of course he had no notion I was in my nightgown! Like an idiot I accepted.

"We got there and the room was jammed with people and TV lights, 1966 TV lights, so it was hot as it could possibly be. Everybody kept offering to take my coat. 'No, no, no, I'm fine,' I insisted, 'I'm just fine. I'm from the South and oh, it's cold.' Then my friend asked me to lunch and at that point I had brains enough to go home. No lunch. I think I might have even mentioned to him that I was in my nightgown. It does show you that I was a basket case. I guess I didn't even realize how much of a basket case."

Eventually she found a job writing for a small publication called *The Insider's Newsletter*. "I became a much happier human being," she wrote, and her feistiness returned. One day she overheard me talking to a friend about commuting to work. The West Side was convenient for us, I noted, because of where the *Times* was located. But if I worked, say, at *Esquire* magazine, which was on Madison Avenue, of course we'd move to the East Side. "In randomly picking a building as an example, he had unthinkingly chosen the exact place where I worked," she later recalled. "It was one of those sensitive male moments. And yes, getting to my job was a pain in the neck." One morning we were jarred awake by a phone call. It was an operator asking if we knew anyone in Oberlin, Ohio, who may have called us. No, said Cokie, we didn't. After she hung up, I protested, yes, we do—my brother lives there. "I know that," she replied tartly, "but I'm not going to help out the phone company." Since her commute was a "pain in the neck," she then got up and went to work. I was still home when the phone rang again. "This is the operator," said an accusing female voice, "did you lie to us this morning when you said you didn't know anybody in Oberlin?" No, I protested, that was my wife, and I started to spell her name. Of course it was Cokie calling, and she burst out laughing. I was busted, and she was back to her old mischievous self.

Cokie didn't just want to be a wife, she wanted to be a mother too. As soon as possible. "I was dying for children," she wrote.

"All my life I had wanted children. I loved playing with babies. I loved dolls. I had a great time with my nieces and nephews. We took a trip to Europe after we had been married for a year— Rome, Paris, London in that order—so we were in Rome for our first anniversary. We went someplace for supper in Rome and then to St. Peter's Square with a bottle of Asti Spumante to celebrate our anniversary. And I ruined the whole evening by crying and saying I wanted a baby." But she couldn't ruin the deeper meaning of that anniversary—after five years of uncertainty we were now headed into the future together. I have a card she gave me to mark the date. On the front is a painting by one of our favorite artists, Marc Chagall, of a couple embracing. On the back she wrote out a little verse that I had once composed for her: *"Each day / Is the anniversary / Of a day / On which we loved each other / A little more / Than the day before."*

Parenthood was not the only issue causing us pain in those days. There was also the Vietnam War, and the possibility of my getting drafted. Generational conflicts over the war tore many families apart, but for the Boggses, the tension was especially acute. Cokie's father was a strong ally of President Johnson's, and one day she and her sister, Barbara, had lunch with their parents at 21, a prominent New York restaurant. "We got into a screaming yelling fight about Vietnam," Cokie recalled, with her father saying I should be proud to serve my country by fighting and even dying there. At that point the two sisters stormed out as the other diners, who couldn't help but overhear their squabble, applauded in approval. Afterward Cokie called her friend Marcia

Burick and "she was weeping," Marcia recalled. "Had she ever had a conversation like that with her father? It was really a watershed, wasn't it? I think this was the first time she had ever confronted him." If she had to choose, Cokie told Marcia, she would choose "my husband over my father and it will always be that way."

I had been avoiding the draft by attending graduate school at night, but the pressures were growing—from Cokie to have a baby and from my draft board to find a more durable solution. Parenthood seemed to be the answer to both problems and we even joked that we'd name the child Lewis Hershey Roberts, after the head of the draft system. It turns out we both misread the law. If you had a grad school deferment past a certain date, you no longer qualified for a fatherhood deferment, but by the time we realized our mistake, Cokie was happily and hugely pregnant. That summer we attended the Democratic convention in Chicago, where protestors shouted with anger and policemen shook with anxiety. "My 'condition' turned out to be a great advantage in the end because I was very thin and from the back you couldn't tell that I was pregnant," Cokie wrote. Whenever a cop tried to poke her in the back and move her along, "I finally learned to swing around in my full pregnant glory and declare, 'Do it again and I'm going to have this baby right here right now.' It worked! A very useful weapon."

Cokie was determined to try natural childbirth, without anesthesia, and we attended classes that summer to prepare for the delivery. I had also contracted with *Good Housekeeping* magazine to write a first-person account of the process, which would pay the bills. On Saturday, October 19, the due date was still a week or two away. Cokie spent the day painting a dresser bright blue, and I screwed on sixteen little yellow-and-red knobs. She took a nap and woke up feeling lousy. Then she cooked a nice dinner but didn't eat it—never a good sign. By midnight we realized she was in labor. I grabbed all the gear we were supposed to bring to the hospital and dislodged a bottle of turpentine with my elbow. After we spent fifteen minutes cleaning up the mess we headed out and hailed a cab. Cokie was doing the breathing exercises that alleviated the pain of her contractions, and the driver seemed less than thrilled with his panting passenger. "Don't worry," I assured him with false confidence, "she won't have the baby in your car." And she didn't. The delivery went smoothly, for the most part. One piece of equipment you're supposed to bring is a paper bag, so the mother can breathe into it and avoid hyperventilating. I had picked one from the fish store—not a good choice under the circumstances. Since I was writing an article, I had also packed a notebook, and in between gasps she demanded at one point, "Is that notebook sterile?" Lee Harriss Roberts arrived at about two thirty, healthy and howling. I went to call my parents, told them their first grandchild had been born, and returned to Cokie's room. She was sitting up in bed, far too elated to sleep, but in typical fashion, already planning the next day and directing my actions. "When you come tomorrow," she said, "bring me a corned beef on rye and a beer." After the *Good Housekeeping* article appeared, readers kept telling me how brave I'd been to witness the birth of our baby. Those comments, as you can imagine, did not sit well with the new mom. "Gee, Steven, did it hurt much?" she would crack. "How about those stretch marks?"

The next day I brought Cokie and the baby home from the hospital, got them settled in the apartment, and went down to the *Times* office. As I walked in the door, my editor called me over and delivered a bombshell: "We want to send you somewhere." I asked quickly: "Where? Washington?" My dream was to return there as a reporter, but the *Times* had another—and better—idea. "No," he answered, "Los Angeles." Now, I had been west of the Mississippi for exactly one day in my entire life, so I was not thrilled with the idea. But Cokie was always more adventuresome than I was and eager for the opportunity. Besides, the youth culture was exploding as a story, and the *Times* reporters on the West Coast were all in their fifties. I was being handed the best possible assignment. That night as I walked home I bought two books that symbolized our new life. One was *Dr. Spock's Baby and Child Care*. The other was Tom Wolfe's *The Pump House Gang*, an ode to the surfing life of Southern California.

The timing could not have been better. Life with a new baby in Manhattan was about to change dramatically. As winter approached and the weather turned, Cokie would pack up and venture out for walks and errands. One day, at the kosher butcher, she panicked, convinced the child—buried under layers of blankets—had stopped breathing. (He hadn't.) "When I tried to take the baby to the pediatrician for his first visit, I stood at Broadway and 75th for half an hour, trying to hail a cab and couldn't get one," Cokie remembered. "Finally, in tears, I went back to the apartment, called the pediatrician and canceled the appointment. I felt like a total failure as a mother. I was plenty happy to leave New York."

A few months later we left Lee with my parents and headed to Los Angeles to find a place to live. I could not have located LA on a map, I was so clueless, and the only name of a hotel I knew was the Ambassador, because Robert Kennedy had been shot there the previous June. The first houses we viewed didn't feel right; they didn't say California. Then we saw an ad in the paper. *Very unusual*, it said, *not for everyone*, so we were intrigued and called the owner. She gave us directions, I saw the Pacific Ocean for the first time, we drove seven miles up the coast and turned into the hills. As we kept climbing, we looked at each other and said, "Are we out of our blooming minds?" Finally we got to the last house on the top of the hill, but since the driveway approached from the rear we couldn't see what was on the other side. When the owner arrived and opened the door, at our feet was a totally unimpeded view of the entire Santa Monica Bay, looking back toward LA. We turned to each other and said, "We'll take it." We didn't know the rent, or how many bedrooms it had, but this was what we'd been looking for. This was California. A few months later we packed up the baby and headed west. I had turned twenty-six, and when we arrived, I had a notice from my draft board saying they were no longer interested in me. And as we changed his diaper for the first time in our new house, Lee laughed. Our little family was ready for a new life.

Over the years, Cokie's identity as a wife never faltered, but it did change—dramatically—and so did my role as her husband. By 1993, she had become a genuine star, and the *Washington Post* magazine did a cover story about her headlined, "Roberts Rules" and beginning, "One day you look up and Cokie Roberts is everywhere—on the radio, on TV, on the talking heads circuit." By 1996, she was anchoring ABC's Sunday-morning show, and in 1998 she had started a whole new career as a popular book author. Now she had a much bigger audience and a much bigger income than I did, and inevitably that created conflicts. "There were some fairly dramatic conversations where I would announce, 'I'm quitting. This is not worth it,'" she recalled. "There has never been any question in my mind about what the priority is here. Let's make that clear." In *We Are Our Mothers' Daughters*, she wrote this about me: "Once he told me that he felt like he was another item on my list of things to do. Ouch, that struck home. What kind of wife was that?"

No marriage is perfect; we were both fallible people who made mistakes. One of my biggest came in 2002, after she was diagnosed with breast cancer. Chemotherapy was causing her hair to fall out, and one day she just shaved it all off, and when I came home that night she was in the kitchen, making dinner and wearing a turban on her head. I was devastated. No matter how hard I tried, I could not hide my dismay, or avoid upsetting her deeply. Another mistake of mine, which I made for many years, was to get irritated when Cokie would interrupt me—which she did often. That led to some nasty spats, sometimes in front of friends, who would cringe in discomfort. Then I interviewed the linguist Deborah Tannen on a radio show, who said this was a common problem between men and women because they approach conversations differently. Men often see them as competitions, while women see them as a cooperative endeavor, and when they interrupt, they think they're helping. "That's the way we talk," Cokie has written. "We're constantly interrupting and going off on a path and coming back. We all know what we're doing. It's a completely different language from the one men speak. So, when Steven read this book, it hit him in the face—hey, this is what we've been arguing about all these years. She's just acting like a girl."

Religion was not the only difference in the way we were raised. Cokie came from a large Southern public family where distant cousins and visiting constituents were always welcome—for a meal, a bed, a tour of the capitol. My upbringing was very different—a Northern immigrant private family crammed into one floor of a two-family house with no room or instincts to accommodate guests. Cokie called this difference "the biggest source of tension in our marriage" and explained: "There are times when I feel Steven is being selfish, when he doesn't want to put himself out. Other times I know he is absolutely right, that if we operated the way I would instinctively operate, we would never have a minute to ourselves, we would be completely overtaken by other people's demands. But there are still times when I think he's wrong."

One great source of stability in our marriage was the house we moved into when we finally returned to Washington in 1977.

Cokie had picked it out when she was eight, telling her dubious mother that her father would buy it for her (he did). At first, she hated the idea of living in her hometown, let alone the house she grew up in. But eventually she came to cherish the sense of continuity and community the old homestead represented. Her parents lived there twenty-five years, then we had more than forty-two years together, and I'm still in residence, keeping the house alive as the center of a vast extended family. Five other weddings have taken place in the garden since ours in 1966—including our daughter, my brother, and a niece—plus countless events marking holidays celebrated, birthdays remembered, engagements announced, books published, honors won, deaths mourned. The man who tents over the patio for those rituals finally left all his hooks and anchors in place, as he knew there would always be another party at Bradley Boulevard. I planted four small crepe myrtle trees that were decorations at our daughter, Becca's, wedding, and more than twenty-four years later they stand tall and strong at the entrance to our driveway. "I realized," Cokie eventually conceded, "Steven had been right to come home."

I give Cokie most of the credit for keeping us on an even keel. There was never any question about her priorities, and she never once used her growing celebrity or income as leverage in our relationship. (Okay, maybe once, when we renovated the house and created a large new dressing room for her that included, as I used to joke, "drive-in closets.") Still, I had to do a lot of thinking and a lot of adjusting. When the *Washington Post* magazine published that cover story on Cokie, the writer interviewed me at length and wrote, "You spend two hours talking to him and what becomes clear is he's very proud of his spouse, a spouse who's become in the last several years far more prominent than he is. Of course, it causes problems." I've often been asked how I handled Cokie's celebrity and I've tried to be candid about those difficulties. We were in the same business. I would have been delighted to join the Sunday roundtable on ABC or analyze politics on Monday morning for NPR. And men of my generation were not brought up to see their spouses as professional equals—let alone as "far more prominent." But many years ago I came to peace with her prominence. Jealousy is a virus that could have easily infected our relationship. I was determined not to let that happen and so was she. Besides, I was Cokie's biggest fan. I was attracted to her in the first place because she was so smart and strong, and I was not surprised when the rest of the world discovered what I had always known about her. In fact, I was less astonished at her success than she was. "At the core, things have not changed at all," I told the *Post.* "What has changed is the world's perception of us."

We were well aware of that perception and tried very hard to keep things in perspective. After we published a bestselling book in 2000 about our marriage, *From This Day Forward*, we were interviewed on CNN and host Wolf Blitzer went way overboard, calling us Washington's "premier power couple." When we came home that night, our aging basset hound, Abner, had pooped all over the kitchen floor. As we got down on our hands and knees, scrubbing away, we turned to each other and said, "How does it feel to be Washington's premier couple now?" If we were ever tempted to let that celebrity stuff go to our heads—and we were not—Abner had provided the perfect antidote.

We always tried to live by a pretty simple set of rules, and one of them was "take the first plane home." We both traveled a lot but were committed to minimizing the time away. In a column for *Town & Country* magazine, we described some of our other adages: "Make time for each other. We both have a lot of obligations, and it would be easy to go days without sharing a meal or a conversation." When we were both working at home, we would email each other from our separate studies saying, "Are you ready for lunch?" When we were out of the house we would talk many times a day, just to say: "How did your class go?" or "The daffodils are out in Rock Creek Park!" or "Have you heard from the kids?" When one of us was away we had an agreement: call when you get in, no matter how late. We were married for more than nineteen thousand days, and we failed to talk to each other on only a handful of them. These days I miss Cokie the most at those small moments when we'd always check in: just before class, or when I'm heading home from school or tennis. I'm still tempted to call and say, "I'm running late" or "Can I pick anything up?" And I still hear her voice saying, "I can't wait to see you." When I hear my phone, with the same ringtone I've had for years, I think it's her calling. Her name is still the first listing on my speed dial, and I cannot bear to erase it.

Another incident provided a particularly useful watchword. After Cokie had been interviewed by a well-known anchor, he demanded that she retape the conversation because she had talked a little too long. Here was a man who appeared on national TV almost every night, and he was bickering about a few seconds of airtime. Cokie and I discussed it later and wondered: "How much is enough?" There will always be someone else who is on TV more often, who makes more money or turns more heads or owns more shoes—whatever metric of success matters to you. And if you are always competing, and are never content, you condemn yourself to a state of eternal dissatisfaction. We always told each other we had more than enough, because we did.

In late 2017, the *New York Times* interviewed us for a regular column they run about marriage, and that gave us both a chance to reflect on our long years together. Here's an edited version of what they published:

Mrs. Roberts: *Enormous changes happened during our marriage. Steve had to do a lot of accommodating and adapting. I had to learn that was not easy for him to do. I just expected it, that he would change, and that was not kind. Change is hard. I keep threatening to needlepoint a pillow in a Victorian style that says "Change sucks."*

The key in marriage is to try to change together. Couples don't have to change at the same time, it's more a question of getting there if you want to have that connection and commitment. There are different paces, and you have to realize that, and accommodate each other.

Then there's resiliency. I always had two jobs and was raising a family. You're so frantic and stressed, all you can do is

get through the day . . . I wasn't always able to appreciate him;
and he, me. We've learned to do that more now that we're old.
We understand what we have is really important. We were crazy
nuts about each other. We still are.

Mr. Roberts: *In a healthy relationship, at the core of lon-*
gevity is a mutual respect and a sense of equality. Biting your
tongue is often the right reaction to a moment of passing anger.
Candor is overrated. I don't mean deception or secrets. I mean
real mutual respect, which leads to being gentle, loving, cautious
and careful at times. It leads to being silent and having self-
restraint, which really helps get you through difficult moments.
There's understanding that if you say everything that comes to
your mind, at every moment, in the name of being honest, it's
often self-indulgent and hurtful.

In a really good marriage you learn from each other. You see
each other's strengths and virtues and when it really works, you
adopt them as your own. One of the great joys of a long marriage
is what you've meant to each other, and held each other up, and
been at each other's side.

More than a year before that article was published, we had celebrated our fiftieth wedding anniversary, on the exact spot where
we'd been married, in the garden of Cokie's childhood home. It
was a joyous night, filled with family and old friends, but one
clouded by bad news. After fourteen years, Cokie's cancer had
returned. Her doctor made it clear there was no cure. New drugs
were available that could hopefully keep the disease at bay, but

we both knew the likely outcome: she would have three more years. We tried to live a normal life, and usually we did. She told very few people because she adamantly did not want to be defined by her illness. And as she often remarked, it's hard enough being a woman in your seventies on TV, it's even harder if folks see you as "sick." She imposed a strict rule: "No sighing, no crying" while I was around her. So I did my crying in the car. As usual, she was thinking about others, trying to shield me from the darkness that was closing in on us, but she confided her fears to her female friends. "She would describe her physical situation and what was going on inside of her, but not in a 'poor me' way at all," said her confidant Robin Sproul. "The science of it, the reality of it, the outlook of it, where she found hope. But she just kept saying, it's devastating. It's devastating. I'm not surviving this. It's a question of when. And she told me she was terribly worried about how you would do after she died, the emotional toll on you and also just getting by every day, picking up all the pieces, picking up the things that she did." She'd reveal her sadness to me at times, especially when she was around the grandchildren, because they reminded her so poignantly of what she would miss—their adult lives. Her sister had died at fifty-one, her mother at ninety-seven, and she would sometimes say wistfully, "I thought I would get the Maw Maw card," using the family's pet name for Lindy. Years before, Cokie had promised Regan, our oldest grandchild, that she'd speak at her high school graduation in May of 2019. As the date approached, her cancer was taking hold and weakening her body, but not her determination. She obsessed over keeping her promise and managed to make the speech, four months before she died. Just days before she went into the hospital for the last time, she insisted on speaking at a fundraiser, honoring the husband of a colleague who had died of cancer. And she had lunch with the daughter of Jon Karl, her colleague at ABC, to counsel her about career plans.

All that summer I could feel her fading, and we told each other many times a day how much we loved each other. One day she said to me, "I just feel awful," and I knew it was serious because she never said things like that. She entered the hospital and said to her doctor, Stan Lipkowitz, "Are we out of options?" He answered no, there were still therapies to try. "Will you tell me when we're out of options?" she asked. And he said yes, he would. On her last weekend, she was still thinking about others first. She emailed our friend Gloria Borger, telling her how sorry she was to miss the wedding of Gloria's son. At seven thirty p.m. on September 13, just hours before she lost consciousness, she told an author who requested an interview: "Of course I remember you. I would be delighted to talk to you. So just let me know what works for you." She was fighting an infection that had left her very weak, and I got a call, early on the morning of Saturday the fourteenth, from the hospital. Her organs were starting to fail, and she was in intensive care. She lasted three more days, but when the doctors told us there was no hope of recovery, we decided to take her off life support. There was nothing left unsaid between us. We were still "crazy nuts" about each other. I held her hand as she died.

Mother

"My first definition of self has been 'mother.'"

Cokie's public celebrity never altered her personal value system. She always placed family first. "No matter what else I've ever done," she wrote, "my first definition of self has been 'mother.'" That doesn't mean she disdained work; she embraced it. She wrote in *We Are Our Mothers' Daughters* that staying home "would have been a disaster" for her. But there's no contradiction here. For Cokie, work and home didn't clash with each other, they reinforced each other. "I need to work for my spiritual and emotional well-being, and while that might not be admirable, it's true," she wrote. "In interim periods between jobs I've suffered genuine depression, and believe me, that's not good for the children. I was a better mother because I worked."

It was still true, Cokie wrote, that "in those days, the roles could not have been more clear. Steven's work came first." But we'd both learned how important it was for her to have a separate identity and a measure of independence. Her first job in Washington after college had involved producing a high school quiz show, *It's Academic*, and just as we were moving west, her old boss had sold the show to the NBC affiliate in Los Angeles. "It worked out perfectly for everyone to have me produce the show out there," she noted. "It gave me something to do, someplace to go, some people to meet, and some checks to cash."

In May of 1970, the *Los Angeles Times* wrote an article about the show, and Cokie told the reporter: "I think of the time I spend on my job as time I need for myself." Even then she was thinking about the themes she later refined in many of her books, speeches, and interviews. She and her contemporaries went to high school in the '50s and college in the '60s, and those very different experiences created a tension: "I think the challenge to this type of woman lies in how to achieve balance between her family and herself. On one hand we were educated in good schools to contribute to the world—our husbands married us because we were that way. On the other hand, we were brought up to believe that a husband and family were terribly important."

Cokie (the *Times* actually referred to her as "Cogie") described that balancing act in concrete terms. "The second I put the baby down for a nap, I rush over to the typewriter" and work on the show, she said. "I need two hours of concentration time and that's about how long the baby sleeps. What falls by the wayside is my house. But I don't have a husband who cares if the rugs need vacuuming. It's much easier to work if you have a husband who believes in women working." But change came slowly, as she wrote later: "Women like me were beginning to voice complaints about our unequal roles, to stir up family arguments on the subject. Men like Steven were defensive on one hand, trying to adapt on the other, taking on more childcare when it was convenient and even washing a dish or two."

Yes, I was washing a dish or two, but I was still stuck in a traditional mindset. "Though he tried to be helpful, Steven was still fairly clueless about this baby business," Cokie wrote. "I remember at one point some friends were considering whether to have a baby, and I heard Steve say, 'Oh, you should do it. It hasn't changed our lives a bit.' 'What?' I exploded. 'It seems to me that everything I'm doing now I didn't do before, and everything I used to do I'm not doing now! I would call that changing my life!'" One incident sums up the conflict between the two roles women like Cokie were now playing. Four months after the *Los Angeles Times* piece appeared, our second child, Rebecca, was born. She came very quickly, and we barely made it down the mountain and to the hospital in time. Cokie joked that my reflexes, honed by years on the basketball court, helped me catch her as she appeared. The obstetrician, who had gone back to sleep after our first warning call, always claimed he had made it in time for her feet. Not quite. Cokie's mother came out to help, and when the baby was a few days old, a fierce brushfire forced us to evacuate and move into a downtown hotel. Becca had arrived early, Cokie had scheduled tapings of her TV show that could not be postponed, and she recounted what happened: "So, I left the ten-day-old and the two-year-old with my mother in a hotel room and went to work. Mamma said, 'When I had a ten-day-old I was still in the hospital.' I, oh so thoughtfully, shot back, 'Take her to the hospital if you want, I have to go to work.' That's the way it was. If you worked you accommodated. There was never any question of the workplace or the family accommodating you." A year or two later, NBC hired Cokie to produce another show, called *Serendipity*, which took kids on field trips around the LA region. Her producing credit on the show said "Cokie Roberts," but when it won a local Emmy award, her certificate read, "Mrs. Stephen Roberts." They couldn't see her as a professional apart from her husband—and then couldn't even spell her name right! At least they didn't call her "Cogie."

While she was taping her shows at the NBC affiliate in Burbank, Cokie met a fellow named Tom Brokaw, who was anchoring the nightly news at the same station. "I would see her at Burbank and she was always getting ready to do something else," Tom told me. "She had her own show and then she was also a mother and she was doing all this other stuff and running the household as well. I do remember thinking, God, she's got a lot on her plate." Tom's wife, Meredith, was performing a similar juggling act, and as he puts it, "These women were changing the world on the fly."

Cokie's female friendships were always deeply important to her, but moving across the country had unplugged her old high school and college connections, and as a new mom in a new place she was eager to forge new relationships. At a birthday party for a two-year-old, Cokie met Millie Harmon, the wife of a young lawyer and the mother of three small daughters. "I remember being introduced to both of you, but mainly to Cokie, and she and I just clicked right away," Millie recalls. "She didn't have a core of friends out here at all, and so I think what I brought to her was an introduction to the community that became much of your community here." The women became even closer after Millie's husband, Ellis, was killed in a rafting accident a year later. Since I was traveling a lot, they would take the kids to the park and then to dinner "and fill them with all those horrible things that nobody's supposed to eat anymore, hamburgers and fries and all that stuff," Millie recalls. Millie herself had grown up in Southern California, but her parents had been refugees from Nazi Germany, and many of the people she introduced us to were transplants from other places, and missing their families and friendship networks as much as we were. "We created our family, and family holidays, for where we were in our new lives," says Millie. Both women found it amusing that Cokie, the Catholic, took over the

Jewish holiday of Passover, and Millie, who is Jewish, organized Easter. We also had many family dinners together with squads of small children running around, and wine was always a key component of those evenings. To one event at our house, the Brokaws, who were from South Dakota, brought boxes of raisins to entertain the kids. As the evening wore on and the little ones got bored, they started stomping the raisins into our living room rug. The adults were too inebriated to protest much, and one of us remarked wearily, "I guess the raisins were a bad idea." That's been a family saying ever since to describe a good intention gone seriously wrong.

This was the early '70s in Southern California, the new age of sex, drugs, and rock and roll, and restraints and relationships were collapsing all around us. To make it worse, most of us were separated from the support structures back home—family, church, community—that expected young couples to stay married and helped ensure that they did. My travels often left Cokie alone with the kids on our mountaintop, and even though she had a new job and new friends, she still felt isolated and inferior at times. "She was definitely Second Hand Rose," in Millie's words, and frustrated about "not finding her own voice." I was trying to take more responsibility, often caring for the kids on weekends when Cokie had to work, but that was a small drop in a very large bucket. As she's written: "The whole understanding we had was that his work mattered more than anything. But it was beginning to get to me more and more. Steve worked at home when he wasn't on the road and I was supposed to somehow keep these babies quiet and out of his hair. I was exhausted from it all. I used to joke that everybody in California was fantasizing about sleeping with everybody else, and I was fantasizing about sleep, period. When I flew to Miami to join Steven for the Democratic Convention in Miami in 1972, I didn't want to get off the plane. It was the first time I'd had to myself in months."

Cokie confided her fears to Millie—that our marriage would follow so many others that careened off the rails in those years. "It's probably the most vulnerable thing that I knew about her, where she didn't feel any control," Millie recalls. We both believed strongly that we were able to survive because we remained "crazy nuts" about each other. But also because we had fought through some very difficult issues when we were very young. We knew we could do it, we wanted to do it, and we worked hard at staying together. One weekend we left the kids and went by ourselves to San Francisco. Walking along the waterfront to dinner, Cokie turned to me and said, "Have an affair with your wife." It was priceless advice that I've never forgotten.

I wrote a series on divorce for the *Times*, mainly because so many of the couples we knew were separating and I wanted to understand what was happening. A very shrewd therapist said to me, "if you wake up every day and say, why should we stay together today, there are going to be days, there are going to be weeks, there are going to be months when you say, hey, I don't have a good reason." The key to surviving those periods of doubt, he said, is remaining committed to the relationship over a long period of time. And that's what we did and how we felt. There was never a time when our marriage was in serious trouble, but Cokie, in typical fashion, added a note of reality: "But there were times when we were ready to kill each other."

One of those times, when homicide became a real option, occurred when I decided the whole family would rent an RV and drive around the West in the summer of 1971, staying at campgrounds while I wrote a series of stories about Americans on the road. We were discussing my plan at a dinner party one night with Carl Reiner, the comedian, and Tom Brokaw remembers that Reiner turned to Cokie and said, "'Here's the deal. You get two big bottles of whatever you like to drink and have them at your side the entire trip.' It was hilarious." For Reiner maybe, not for Cokie. "First of all," she later wrote, "it's important to understand, I think the outdoors is vastly overrated. I am not an outdoor person. When we got in this camper the thing smelled to high heaven, just start there. Then we forgot to lock the refrigerator door, so as we pulled out of the driveway, the food all spilled out. I did more housework in that stupid camper than I did at home for a year." There were no bathtubs and the kids were too small for showers, so they never really got clean. Becca wasn't even a year old, she was still in diapers, and as Cokie recalls, "By the time I got her dressed, and turned around to get my purse, she was dirty again." I was usually off doing interviews, so Cokie had to amuse the kids by herself, and one day at a county fair she took them on a Ferris wheel. For a long time after that, she had nightmares about Becca trying to crawl out of her seat and plunge to earth. I only found out years later that at every stop along the

way, Cokie had made reservations to fly home. She never followed through, but she never fully forgot her grudge either.

In October of 1972, Cokie's father came through Los Angeles
on his way to Alaska, where he was committed to campaigning
for a fellow member of Congress. "Daddy took the kids swim-
ming in his hotel pool," she wrote. "He spent a nice long day
with them and me. That was the last time I ever saw him." Hale
and his colleague were late for a fundraising event and the pilot
tried to fly through a storm. They never arrived and the wreck-
age of the plane was never found. I was in my downtown office
when my desk in New York called with the news that his plane
was missing. I made an unwise decision and thought I could get
home to tell Cokie in person. But of course, many of our friends
were journalists and they started calling her. Brokaw was one of
them and remembers, "She always said to me later, 'Every time
they say Tom Brokaw's on the phone for you, I get a chill because
I remember that night.' I hesitated about whether I should call
or not but I thought it's better that she hears from me than on
television or somewhere else. I always felt it was kind of a bond
between us." When I finally got home she was standing in the
kitchen weeping—while feeding the children.

Cokie immediately flew east to be with her family. Then they
all decided to go to Alaska while a massive search for the plane
took place. Millie and I took the kids to Disneyland to celebrate
Lee's fourth birthday while Cokie was still away, hoping for news
that never came. "When I finally realized that I would never see
my father again, I was so profoundly sad, I think it was hard for

Steven," she remembered. "I was the youngest child and my father had always taken great delight in me. Losing him meant that never again would I be loved in quite that way. And knowing he would never know my children broke my heart. No matter how much I intellectually accept the fact that the plane must have gone to the bottom of the cold, deep Prince William Sound, emotionally I've always half expected my father to turn up someday. For years, after I moved into the family house, I didn't change the kitchen wallpaper because I was afraid, he might find his way home and then think strangers were there."

We loved living in California, but after five years it was time for a new adventure. In October of 1973, a year after Hale's plane had disappeared, I was in New York, talking to my bosses. And as usual, Cokie had to cope with a crisis by herself: another brushfire threatening our house. It was just before Halloween, and when she decided to pack up and flee to Millie's, the kids insisted on wearing their costumes. "When we got to a police checkpoint on the Pacific Coast highway, off to the left was a huge wall of fire; it looked like the holy card of hell," she later wrote. When the cop on duty checked the car's occupants he found a witch, a ghost, and Freddy the dog. "At least it gave him one good laugh on a terrible night."

The *Times* assigned us to Athens, and we tried to make the kids feel good about their new home by showing them pictures of Greece, including the ruins on the Acropolis. Becca, who had just turned three, said to me in tears, "Daddy, are we going to have to live in one of those tumbled down houses?" On our way we stopped in London for several days, and Cokie always teased me that she had to break an appointment with NBC, to discuss doing some freelance work, because I insisted on going to Burberry to buy a trench coat suitable for a foreign correspondent. I don't quite remember it that way, but there was still no question whose work was more important. And when we got to Greece it was up to Cokie—again—to get the kids and the house settled while I was preoccupied with my new assignment.

We found a lovely home to rent, surrounded by olive and citrus trees, in a convenient neighborhood. It was across the street from where the former military dictator, Georgios Papadopoulos, had once lived, and Cokie wrote to her friend Cinda Perlman, "There's a policeman there with nothing to do that I'm thinking of hiring as a babysitter." But it took a while for our household goods to arrive, and we spent our first weeks in Athens crammed into a small apartment hotel. "We are not yet in because our furniture was put on the Nina or Pinta or Santa Maria, so the four of us are in two rooms in the middle of downtown Athens and driving each other wild," Cokie wrote with characteristic wit. "Lee only goes to school in the mornings, so he has all afternoon to pick on Becca and make her scream. There's not much to do about it since the whole city, including most playgrounds, closes down for siesta, which I can't convince anyone around here to take except me." She detested not working and confided to her friend, "There's really not much for me to do. I've bought the only things I could for the house before moving in, measured for curtains etc. about ½ dozen times and checked out the nursery schools." The tension she described back in California had not gone away. She relished being a mother, but not *just* a mother. "It's been a long time since I've done full-time mothering and I hate it," she admitted. "I think I must be ill-suited for the job."

Not long after she wrote that letter, Cokie got some relief from "full-time mothering" when CBS started asking her to file radio reports about the turbulent Greek political scene. But her main job was still managing our household in a foreign country without a lot of modern conveniences that Americans took for granted. And I could not possibly have done my job without her wholehearted support. She loved to tell the story about buying a little grill and searching for charcoal, which she eventually discovered was sold at lumberyards. All they would sell her was a huge bag, so when she got it home, she kept driving over it in the car to break up the fuel into usable chunks. "Accomplishments like that, as minor as they were, gave me a wonderful sense of competence," she later wrote. "I didn't need Steven to do those things; in fact, he would have told me I was nuts to drive over the charcoal, but it worked." In *We Are Our Mothers' Daughters*, she summarized an important lesson: "In those years I found out something new about this wife business—or maybe more accurately, the husband side of that coin. By having to do everything myself I found out that I was actually a highly competent human being. I didn't need Steven around, I wanted him around. Life was a lot more fun with him than without him. Emotionally I had not the slightest desire to manage on my own, but practically I could do it. That was a revelation. (I did think it was a little much, though, one day when Steve and the landlord sat in the living room drinking brandy while I was in the basement fixing the furnace.)"

Even though she sometimes resented the burdens of "full-time mothering," Cokie understood how much the children contributed to our lives in Greece. "We had a completely different experience living in a foreign country with children than we would have without children," she reflected. "From my perspective as a woman alone a lot of the time, children forced me out of my innate shyness. I *had* to go to the park. I *had* to go to the school. I needed to form a community for the children's sake. I would hate to have to move to a new place without children. For women particularly, I think, the universality of mothers in a park is enormous. It doesn't matter what language anyone speaks, we all respond in the same way when a child falls."

As a woman on her own so often, she had to master Greek traffic—and parking. Since no self-respecting Greek would ever pay a ticket, the cops resorted to a more devilish approach—they removed your license plates if you parked in an illegal spot. After that happened to her once, and retrieving the plates had taken half the day, she went on one of her rants: "It had me completely crazy. I was not ever going to let that happen to me again." One day she was dashing into my office, and all the spots reserved for foreign press cars were taken, so she parked illegally, for just a few minutes, but when she returned a cop had removed her plates. The tale continues: "I tried reasoning with him. Hah! Then I started shouting, 'Let's go to the Ministry of Information right now!' He growled a few words, then ignored me. So I put the children in his car and climbed in after them. Lee flipped through a stack of plates on the floor and pointed, 'Here's our license plate right here.' By this time I had certainly succeeded in getting the cop's attention. He kept ordering me out of his car. I refused, leaving him with the choice of dragging a woman and two children out onto the street or giving me my license plate back." Finally the cop backed down and returned the plate. "It was a wonderful moment," Cokie recalled, "because the children went between thinking this was the most fun thing they had ever done in their lives and being totally terrified that we were all going to go to jail because of their crazy mother. But they were on my team. They were pretty good about hanging in there with me."

Yes, they were. Since I was traveling so much, the three of them had to do a lot of things without me, and one year, Cokie took the kids by herself to Rosh Hashanah services, marking the Jewish New Year, run by the American military at a hotel near the airport. She told what happened: "The military would bring in a visiting rabbi and I found him sitting out on the balcony of his room, looking out at the water. I knocked and said, 'Sorry, are there Rosh Hashanah services here?' He explained that at services the night before, the other families had decided not to come back again, but he was hanging around in case anybody showed up. So I said to him, 'Here we are.' The kids were four and six. It was perfect. He pulled out the Torah and let them see it and touch it. Then he pulled out the shofar, the ram's horn that is blown to signal the start of the year. He let them try to blow it and of course they couldn't, but it was a neat thing to try. Then we all went downstairs to this American hotel and the kids had real American ice cream and the rabbi and I had American beers. Happy New Year!"

For a long time, we assumed we'd stay abroad after the Athens assignment; the *Times* had penciled us in to move to Bangkok, and Cokie was ready to go. As she often remarked, she'd become a very good foreign correspondent's wife and wanted to continue in that role. But returning home was what I wanted to do. I'd been traveling heavily for nine years, I was missing much of the children's upbringing, and my aim had always been to work in Washington, where I had first started. So when the new bureau chief, Hedrick Smith, called me one night and offered me a job, I was eager to take it. Cokie, on the other hand, was devastated. "To me, moving to Bangkok seemed like absolutely the right thing to do," she remembered. "On the contrary, moving to Washington seemed like the worst possible thing to do. To me it was like dying. I was coming back to where I grew up. I was thirty-three years old and it was like being buried alive. I didn't want to do it. I remember feeling helpless and blue, and not knowing quite how to get myself out of it." She tells the story of seeing a pretty dress in a store window and thinking that "buying that would give my spirits a boost. But then the dress ended up costing more than I usually spent and that depressed me even more. When I told Steve about it, he stole out and bought me the dress. As silly as it might seem, that made me feel a good deal better. At least he showed he cared, even if he couldn't do much to fix the problem."

Once again, for the fourth and last time, we moved for my job. We'd been gone from Washington for eleven years. I wrote to my parents saying, "We've promised ourselves that Washington is only another assignment, and that two or three or four years from now we'll move on again, hopefully back abroad." But Cokie knew better. She assumed that once we returned, we'd never leave, and she was right. We moved into the house on Bradley Boulevard, the house where she'd grown up and we were married. Lindy, who had replaced Hale in Congress after his death, was living there alone, and she greeted us warmly, giving up her own bedroom and moving in with Becca in Cokie's old room. We started looking for other places to live, but the perfect solution soon became obvious to everybody. We'd buy the house from Lindy, who was then able to afford an apartment downtown closer to the Capitol. Not only did we move into her parents' old room, we even rescued their old bed, an ancient but lovely cherrywood four-poster that had been consigned to the attic. ("Talk about weird," as Cokie once put it.) The kids, now seven and nine, entered the local public school and adjusted well, except for not knowing any of the American TV shows their classmates kept talking about. But they quickly learned to fake it.

Despite her fears, Cokie didn't perish in Washington; she prospered. She found a job at a fledgling news operation called National Public Radio, first as a freelancer and then as a full-time reporter, and as she started working harder and traveling more, all of us had to make adjustments. When the nuclear reactor at Three Mile Island in Pennsylvania partially melted down, NPR sent Cokie there, and she was eager to go. A few hours later, the *Times* asked me to go as well and I refused. It would not be fair to our kids to have both parents away, and in danger. That was the first time that her job took precedence over mine. It wouldn't be the last. Later that year she was covering the visit of Pope John Paul II to the United States, and I got a call at the office from the mother of one of Becca's friends. Becca had fallen and gashed her forehead and they were headed for the emergency room. Could I meet them there? Just as I was putting on my coat the phone rang. It was Cokie saying she was done with the Pope and heading home. Her version: "As he was starting to do a whole guilt number on me, I interrupted him. 'Save the guilt for later, Steven, and just listen to two words: "Plastic surgeon."' He hung up, grumpy, but he did go right home and get her to the doctor."

By the next year we were both covering the national political campaign and traveling constantly, but we figured something out that I have passed on to many of my students and other young parents. The key to sanity is not how many hours you work but who decides which hours you work. And for both of us, that meant writing about voters, not politicians. If you were covering Ronald Reagan, say, and he was giving a speech in Milwaukee on the night your child was singing in a school concert, you missed the concert. But if you were doing a story about the ethnic Catholics in Milwaukee who were switching to Reagan, you could make the concert and go to Wisconsin the next day. Sometimes we leapfrogged each other, staggering reporting trips so one of us was at home. But since we really liked and missed each other, we'd travel together at times, and very keen fans of NPR and the *Times* might have noticed the same voters occasionally appearing in both of our reports. At the end of that campaign we published a joint article in the *Times* magazine, combining everything we'd learned from voters during the previous months, and both of us understood the symbolic importance of what we'd done. We were now professional equals, doing the same jobs, covering the same stories. And as a result, there was one phrase neither one of us could ever say to the other: "You know, dear, you just don't understand."

After the election and Reagan's victory, we were both assigned to Capitol Hill full-time. We loved it! We could commute together, eat lunch together, trade information and contacts and gossip and catch up at the end of the day on the ride back to the suburbs. "By the time we finally got home, the kids had our undivided attention," Cokie recalled. Many of our colleagues knew we were married, but a hot rumor swept the press gallery: Cokie Roberts was having an affair with a *New York Times* reporter! The arrangement also meant, however, that if one of us was working late, odds were that both of us had to stay downtown. We desperately wanted to have dinner with the kids, but they confided to us years later that on many nights when we were delayed, they'd eat early at a friend's house and just pretend to share our meal when we got home. "Our motives were good, but we sometimes made their lives more difficult," Cokie admitted.

And they sometimes made our lives more difficult. Cokie spoke often about her motherly instincts kicking in every afternoon at

about three, when the kids came home from school. She recalls
her work friends "trying to mute their giggles" as they heard her
say sternly into the phone: "Rebecca, you have an obligation to
go to your piano lesson, you've made a commitment. . . . Lee,
stop picking on your sister." But she always took their calls. As
Becca now remembers: "As a working parent sometimes your kid
calls and you don't really have time to talk but she never made me
feel that way. And she must have been on deadline all the time."

Cokie tried hard to emulate her mother's model as "the great
guilt remover" and she told one interviewer that Lindy's man-
tra, "Your kids are doing great," shaped her own parenting style:
"My mother's support for me and for what I was doing was terribly important to me. I would feel very proud of my daughter
and my daughter-in-law under any circumstances because they
are terrific women, but what I learned from my mother is that it's
important to voice it—to tell them what a great job they're doing,
and what terrific kids they have, and how hard I know it is."

Becca, the mother of three boys herself, absorbed that lesson
and followed that lead: "I think Mom's overarching parenting
theory was, always know your kid and know what that kid needs.
Right? And it's not about status or benchmarks or some checklist
that other people think make a successful child. It's about your
kids and they may be different from each other and different
at different ages. The whole goal is to know that kid and that
has been so important to me. Especially as the mother of twins,
you've really got to recognize that they're individuals. Her advice
was almost always trust your judgment, which is great advice,

right? You know your kids, you're doing fine." It wasn't always easy being Cokie Roberts's child, especially her daughter, and Becca says it was "hugely important" that her mother recognized "that your kids are not you and they make choices other than you make and those are still valid. Mom was always really good about that." Becca, our sunnier child, was usually chatty in those afternoon phone calls. Lee not so much, but Cokie remembers other conversations: "Lee would occasionally bare his soul, but only when I was away. He'd see my phone number, call me at one or two in the morning, and pour out his problems. Then he'd go happily to sleep leaving me wide awake in some motel room in Iowa, my arms aching so much to hold him. He told me later that he would never have talked to me so frankly had I been home sleeping in my own bed."

Cokie never tried to sugarcoat the stresses of motherhood. An editor once asked her to write a letter "to her younger self," and her response was revealing: "This kind of absurd mismatch between day-to-day motherhood and the emotional charge it carries can be a little scary. Your kids, like all kids, are a pain in the neck sometimes. As a regular person in your regular life, you really don't get angry. But as a mother, you're shocked at your capacity for anger with your children. Instead of childish misbehavior, their transgressions seem like terrible reflections on you as a mother. Here's my advice about the anger, chaos and isolation. First beware the dangers of extrapolation in motherhood. Despite his impressive tantrums your son will not throw himself on the floor of grocery stores, screaming for candy, when he's grown up. Just because your daughter can't seem to stop talking now, doesn't mean she won't ever. Also, understand this won't last forever. Don't feel oppressed by it. These are very short years in the scheme of things and you will live through them." And sometimes things just clicked. One day during the 1980 campaign Cokie visited Becca's elementary school to talk about her work, wearing a navy-blue suit and bringing her tape recorder to show the kids. A few weeks later was Halloween, and Cokie went "tearing out to Bethesda" in the middle of the day to see the students parading in their costumes: "Flabbergasted, Becca demanded, 'What are you doing here? I don't care about you coming to see the parade.' And I said, 'Well, I care.' It was her last one, her last year in that school. Then, as I looked at the parade, there were all these sixth-grade girls in blue suits with tape recorders! They were dressing up as reporters!"

Despite Cokie's growing professional stature, and responsibilities, being a mother was always at the top of her list. When the kids became teenagers, and posted less-than-perfect driving records, she had a habit of "praying them into the driveway" and could never fall fully asleep until she heard them barge through the back door. We tried hard to make every important event in their lives, but sometimes work did get in the way. Cokie tells this story: "It was the weekend before the 1984 election, I was in Los Angeles, Steve was in Chicago. We each called home to discover that Becca had gone to the homecoming dance. She was a freshman, her date a senior. Lee was decidedly unforthcoming with the details. 'What was she wearing?' I asked. 'Something blue and shiny of yours,' he replied. I felt guilty and angry that I wasn't there, cheated out of my daughter's first dance, worried that no rules had been set with the boy. Steve and I kept calling to check on her. It got later and later, still no Becca. When she finally checked in she explained that she was the last kid in the car to be delivered home because her parents were away and it wouldn't matter." What did matter is that Cokie had missed her only daughter's first date. And she never forgot her failure.

Cokie followed her parents' model. If being the child of public figures had its drawbacks, she felt, it should also have some advantages. In the summer of 1985, Lee was sixteen and working as a page in the House of Representatives. We'd see him all the time, and he loved telling us that he had a message to deliver in the cloakroom off the House floor—a space where he was allowed and we were not. That summer he met a fellow page from California named Liza McDonald, an adorable young woman, spunky and smart, and one evening she came out to the house with us. When we discovered a bat flying around the porch, Liza immediately took charge, driving the creature out with a broom. On the spot, Cokie and I fell in love with this child, and Lee apparently did too—they got married twelve years later.

As the kids finished high school and the empty nest loomed, we weren't quite prepared for the transition. Dropping a child off at college is one of the most indelible moments of parenthood, and when we took Lee to Duke in the fall of 1986, we were struck by the scene in the hotel dining room near campus: most of the tables were occupied by three people, one young, two middle-aged, all radiating anxiety. Two years later, Becca went to Princeton. She had been a model child, hardly ever given to teenage tantrums, but we made a big mistake when we drove her to school. We stayed too late and by the time we departed she could not wait for us to leave. Barely a wave goodbye. We walked off the campus, feeling a bit bruised, and saw a young woman weeping into the arms of her parents. Cokie turned to me and cracked, "Now there's a satisfying child!"

Cokie and Becca had always been close; they sang in the church choir together, and our daughter felt a keen sense of identity, and continuity, with both her mother and grandmother. As she told me: "There are ways we are different. There are ways we are similar. There are values we share. There are places we diverge and what Mom always respected was that I was my own woman. She was very aware of raising a girl in America, raising a girl to be a feminist and raising a girl to believe she could accomplish anything." Cokie later reflected on this turning point in her life: "With Becca going away, I was not only losing my child but my friend. The idea that suddenly this friend wasn't there was shocking. I had prepared for it, but still I was bereft. I couldn't imagine what I would've done if I weren't working as hard as I was. I kept wondering, what did women do when they didn't work and their kids left home? I couldn't wrap my mind around it. I wasn't only missing my kids and seeing big changes in my daily life, I also had to redefine myself. From the moment I had a baby my first responsibility was to those children. I saw my life first and foremost as that of a mother, and suddenly that wasn't my role anymore. At least not in a daily fashion the way it had been for twenty years. I felt almost uprooted."

It was not always easy for our children to establish their own independence and identity, and one story illustrates that tension. After graduating from Duke, Lee spent a year working for the political unit at CBS, where I was subbing regularly as the host of a show called *Nightwatch*. It was on in the middle of the night, so we usually taped during the day, and one Sunday morning in January of 1991, as the Persian Gulf War was dominating the news, I went to CBS to do some interviews. Our friend Lesley Stahl had just finished anchoring *Face the Nation*, and we were chatting in the control room while Lee was answering the phones. I was standing behind him, and in front of him, on a monitor, up pops Mom, who was introducing her own Sunday show. I quickly realized his discomfort, with both parents intruding on his workspace, and retreated to the makeup room. As I heard the story, the room fell silent and all eyes turned to Lee. "Now," he said, "you know why I want to go to law school." The next fall he entered Georgetown, and then went to work for a local law firm, and while he lived downtown with pals he'd come home regularly for Sunday-night dinner and join me at Redskins football games. Eventually he reunited with Liza McDonald, who had gone to journalism school and moved to Washington, and Cokie tells this story: "Lee would bring her over for Sunday dinner and we became great friends. She even worked for me as a research assistant during the 1994 campaign. I kept hoping Lee would do the smart thing and ask her to marry him, then one day he invited me to lunch and I sensed something was up. In the middle of this stuffy dining room he solemnly said, 'I need your advice about diamonds.' I wanted to whoop and hug him and make a big hoopla, but he would have killed me. I didn't know anything about diamonds, but told him where we could go to learn, and then we had to sit through this insufferable food service. Finally lunch ended and I was able to grab him. Then we went jewelry shopping."

Both of our children got married in 1997, only eight weeks apart, and then did exactly what we had done. Move away. Becca and her husband, Dan Hartman, to San Francisco and Lee and Liza to London. It pained us deeply, but we couldn't really complain, since we knew firsthand how important it is for young couples to nurture their relationships without their parents around. As Becca noted, Cokie "was always really good" about letting her children make their own decisions and when I asked for an example she replied: "Moving to San Francisco. Mom hates San Francisco. Precious, provincial and cold. She always wanted a third P to make it cute. The alliteration never worked. It was far away and her mother hen instincts didn't like that very much. But she particularly didn't like that city. I think she would have understood if we moved to LA much more. She'd make snarky comments about it being 40 degrees in June, but she never undermined my faith in my own decision-making ability. When we moved out there, I was 25, I was pretty young, but I was moving on with a very adult life and she absolutely let me make that call."

We were very fortunate on the grandparent front. We had married young and had kids young, and our children also formed families much earlier than many of their contemporaries. Those families were far away, but at least San Francisco and London were great cities to visit. When our first grandchild, Regan, was born—on my fifty-eighth birthday, February 11, 2001—it was a Sunday morning, and Cokie was on the air, hosting her weekly show. As soon as it was over, she insisted that we head straight to the airport and catch the first plane to London. We didn't even stay overnight, but nothing was going to stop Cokie from seeing and holding that baby as soon as possible. Becca was newly pregnant with twins at the time, and seven months later she went into premature labor—again on a Sunday morning. Cokie was on the air when Dan called with the news, and the producer who took the call panicked. Do I tell Cokie while the show is still on— and disrupt her performance? Or wait until the show is over— and upset her for withholding the information? The decision was made to tell her at a commercial break, and the instant she got off the air, she headed for the airport. She was about to board a plane when Dan called to say the delivery had gone well and everyone was fine. This was September 2, 2001, and nine days later, on September 11, Cokie was driving to the airport to return to Washington when the Twin Towers were attacked and all commercial air traffic was halted. ABC finally had to charter a private plane a few days later to get her back to Washington in time to host her show the following Sunday.

Becca recalls that after her boys were born, Cokie kept dropping "not so subtle hints, not as subtle as she thought they were," about how nice it would be to have her daughter and grandchildren back in Washington. "But she always respected that I wanted to come back here on my own terms, that I didn't want to be Cokie and Steve's daughter here, or at least not *only* Cokie and Steve's daughter." When she finally did come back, in the spring of 2006, it was completely on her "own terms," to host a talk show on the local NPR station. She asserted her independence in another way as well, buying a house downtown, not near us in the suburbs, and as she told me, "somehow that five miles down Wisconsin Avenue feels important." The distance felt important to Cokie too, who knew how much her daughter needed space and separation, and Becca never felt her mother was second-guessing her decisions: "We didn't send the kids to public school, we didn't live in the suburbs, we didn't move into Bradley Boulevard, which under some fantasy circumstances you might've thought would've been a nice thing. But it wasn't the right thing for us, and Mom never came here without saying, I love this house."

No mother-daughter relationship is completely free of tension, and Cokie's penchant for passive-aggressive behavior could occasionally irritate Becca (and me): "There was some way she wanted something to go or something she wanted you to do but she was so constitutionally incapable of starting a sentence with the words, 'I want' that she would back around it or suggest it in a way that wasn't really a suggestion. Or try to make you think it was your idea. And once I got on to her about what she was doing, sometimes I'd say okay, that's helpful. But sometimes it would just drive me nuts. Come right out and tell me what you want because this back-alley stuff is maddening."

About the time Becca moved back to Washington, Lee and his family left London for Connecticut, and then settled in North Carolina. Once we had everyone in the Eastern Time Zone, it made sense for us to buy a home in Pawleys Island, SC, a magical place where we had been spending summer vacations for many years. I don't think Cokie was ever happier than when the whole gang gathered at the beach house every June. She had her own rituals with each grandchild, but one of her favorites was getting up very early with the baby, Cecilia, and watching "the big red ball," as they called it, emerge out of the Atlantic Ocean. Cokie delighted in taking her grandchildren with her to interesting places. All six of them accompanied her in different years to the annual White House Christmas party for the press corps. She and Regan, an aspiring artist, spent a week together in Greece. Regan's brother, Hale, attended a joint appearance Cokie made with Joe Biden in New Orleans. Cecilia tagged along when her grandmother spoke in St. Louis to mark the arrival, two hundred years before, of the Sacred Heart nuns in America. Cal, one of Becca's twins, has never quite gotten over a trip to Maine, when Cokie assigned him the job of carrying home a box of live lobsters. Roland, the twins' younger brother, got to meet President George H. W. Bush on another journey to Maine. "I loved when

Mom would just say, sure, you're 11 years old but you can come on this crazy 24-hour trip to Maine with me and we'll figure it out when we get there," said Becca. "And I loved that they wanted to say yes, that they thought taking this crazy trip with their wacky grandma was cool."

CHAPTER THREE

Journalist, the Early Years

"The whim of the moment is TV news broadcasting."

Cokie always had trouble explaining how and why she became a journalist. Since her parents were politicians, reporters were not exactly their favorite people. "We hated the press," she once said. "We thought that reporters got in the way." When the *New York Times* asked, "Whom did you dream of being" as a young girl, she answered: "There was never anybody I wanted to be. I suppose I expected life to be like my mother's. But I did not have some special heroine." Cokie told *Lear's*, "I never had a plan," causing the somewhat flustered writer to conclude: "In a field renowned for sharp elbows and knees, Roberts makes her career sound like a series of happy accidents. Even journalism sounds like an accident—easy to fall into because her husband, Steven, who she married in 1966 at the age of 22, was a reporter." When a radio interviewer asked why she'd become a journalist she answered: "I don't have a good answer to that. It really is that my husband was doing it and it was easier to switch than fight."

There's truth in all those statements, but not quite the whole truth. As a girl growing up in the 1950s, I'm sure it never occurred to Cokie Boggs that her life would turn out the way it did. But by the time she graduated from college in 1964, the world was changing around her and she was becoming a different person. She was starting to understand her own talent and embrace her own ambitions and become the woman who would say, "I need to work for my spiritual and emotional well-being." It took a while for her to figure out exactly what that work would be, but her career in journalism was not completely a "happy accident" either. Her instinct and ability showed up pretty early. When she was graduating from college and browsing through job openings posted at Wellesley, she noticed one for a small TV production company in Washington owned by a woman named Sophie Altman, who had also gone to Wellesley. The business was run out of Sophie's basement—compensation often included a meager lunch—and Cokie's main job was to produce the high school quiz show *It's Academic*. (When Altman died in 2008 at age ninety-five, her *New York Times* obituary said that *It's Academic* was the longest-running quiz show in TV history, according to Guinness World Records.) The show was produced separately in several different cities, and she enjoyed the travel, but days in the Altmans' basement were less enthralling. In March of 1965, she wrote to a college friend, Bob Kaiser, later the managing editor of the *Washington Post*: "My job is OK but really beginning to wear. The traveling has been fun but not very frequent and when I'm home the work is tedious. So I'm in the process of looking for another job." Then she noted, in a remarkably prescient passage, "The whim of the moment is TV news broadcasting but that's much easier said than done. The general response is to go work on a newspaper for five years and then come back. So we shall see." Some whim.

Sophie Altman sensed Cokie's frustration and talent, and not long after that letter was written, created a new show on the NBC affiliate in Washington, WRC, called *Meeting of the Minds*. It was a simple format—Cokie and a panel of reporters interviewed one guest for a half hour on Sunday morning, leading into *Meet the Press* on the NBC network. "It was the Cokie Boggs show, she literally produced it, designed it and moderated it," says her friend and coworker Jean Firstenberg. Cokie wore her hair long in those days, mainly because I loved it that way, but a twenty-one-year-old anchor needed some gravitas, so on the show, she piled it in a bun on the top of her head. That was just a cosmetic change, though. The real Cokie was always there. Sophie Altman was the first but not the last producer to understand that the camera loved her. And she loved it back.

Then we got married and moved to New York where I was working on the city staff of the *New York Times*. She's talked openly about the "genuine depression" she felt in those days as she looked futilely for a job and host Terry Gross of NPR's *Fresh Air* once asked her, "Were you told point blank" they wouldn't hire you "because you were a woman?" Cokie answered with some fury: "Point blank, point blank—we don't hire women to do that. Their voices lack authority. Or we don't hire women writers because men have to work for the writers, and obviously, men can't work for women. I mean, every imaginable thing was said [why] they couldn't hire—you'll leave because you'll get pregnant, all of that. And it was all said straight out loud, and in some ways, it's refreshing because there was no pretense. It was exactly what it is. What they said was what they meant."

Through her college friend Nora Ephron—who was then a reporter in New York—Cokie eventually got the job at *The Insider's Newsletter*. It was her first real taste of journalism, and she later said, "It was essentially reporting and then writing very brief little stories and I loved it." Then the publication folded and she moved to a production job at a local TV station, which she definitely did not love, so she happily quit when she got pregnant with Lee. After we moved west a few months later, she renewed her relationship with Sophie Altman and started producing *It's Academic* in Los Angeles, but she had been bitten by the reporting bug, and her commitment to that profession would last the rest of her life. Our years in New York had taught her some "useful, if painful, lessons," which she summed up this way: "I learned that I need the company of other women. I learned that I perform much better with the discipline of a schedule. And I learned that I derive tremendous satisfaction from my work. I'm not particularly proud of those realizations. I think a more creative and self-contained person would do better on her own. But I'm awfully glad I found out about myself when I did."

California in the late '60s and early '70s was one of the best stories in the entire world. I was deluged with offers to write freelance articles for major magazines, but I was spread very thin, just covering the news for the *Times*, and could not possibly fulfill all the requests. Cokie's TV production work was sporadic, weeks of intense activity followed by periods of idleness, and life on a mountaintop in Malibu with two small children could get pretty lonely, so we hit on a plan. Cokie would research the articles, I'd write them, she'd do the editing, and we'd share a double byline. The plan worked well, we enjoyed collaborating and respected each other's judgment, and we ran into only one small glitch: an article we wrote on a venereal disease pandemic appalled her mother. Cokie later wrote that "Steve became a sort of one-man journalism school for me, generously sharing a byline. Now we do that all the time, but then it was key to my building a body of work. And we were both slowly becoming aware that someday that would make a difference."

Yes, we were becoming aware of her aspirations. And yes, they did make a difference. "It was important to my professional development," she wrote of our joint writing enterprise. "I learned a lot and the public recognition made a huge difference when

we went abroad. It made me feel that I could do something professionally, not be lost." Obviously Cokie couldn't produce TV
shows in Greece, but since she knew that "full-time mothering"
was a recipe for unhappiness, she contacted several broadcast
outlets, offering her services as a part-time "stringer" or freelancer once we got settled in Athens. Getting our house in order
was a painful experience, as Cokie wrote to my parents: "It's bad
enough to deal with plumbers, electricians, etc. in English—in
Greek it's nearly impossible." And she admitted, "I have moments of thinking it will never all happen. The best thing for me
to do is go to work and forget about the house." She got her wish
just days after she wrote those words. She had connected with
CBS, which offered her a chance to do occasional reporting, and
as she had written to my folks just after we arrived: "They gave
me a press card, cassettes, and a thingamajig to hook up your
tape recorder to the telephone so I feel legit. The deal is they'll
try me—and if they like me, I'm on." She had just cabled their
New York office, saying she was ready to start working, when a
right-wing coup in Cyprus deposed the left-leaning government.
For three frustrating days, the airport in Cyprus remained closed
while a platoon of foreign journalists gathered in Athens. Finally
the airport opened and all those correspondents, including me
and the main CBS man in Athens, Dean Brelis, flew to the island.
A day later, the Turks invaded Cyprus and CBS had no one in
Athens to cover the Greek angle of the story. Except Cokie. As
she wrote to Cinda Perlman a few weeks later, "On the morning
of the Turkish invasion CBS called me and asked for a Greek

reaction to the event. Of course, it was 6:30 A.M. and there was no reaction. But they gave me 20 minutes to report and write the first radio spot I had ever done, with no Steven here to help me. And somehow I did it."

Cokie had sprained her ankle, and our friends Jean and Paul Firstenberg, who were visiting us at the time, remember her appearing in the doorway of their bedroom, waving her cane and announcing, "The Turks have invaded and I must go file!" She drove downtown to the Reuters office, which I had been using as a base, and the bureau chief, Neo Tzallas, was already at work. In walked a leading opposition politician, Evangelos Averoff, who later became defense minister, and Cokie was able to put together that first report. "From then on," she wrote to Cinda, "it was round the clock getting out any info I could which wasn't easy because communications were broken down for long periods of time and of course the military junta never gave you any info anyway."

"It was chaos," she recalled years later, "and I didn't know where Steven was. For a little while I didn't know if he was dead or alive until the *Times* got word to me that he was safe. Meanwhile I was filing constantly. The events in Cyprus triggered a reaction in Greece, and the civilian politicians started moving against the military junta. I'd been working twenty-hour days, which was fine because I was so scared about Steve, and it was all very exhilarating." We lived only a few blocks from the Greek Pentagon, just off the city's main north-south avenue, and one day Lee decided to mimic his mother, taking a tape recorder and counting twelve tanks he saw moving down the road. That was big news, and Cokie reported, "According to reliable sources here in Athens, there's been a major movement of tanks through the city." She never said her source was her five-year-old. "Hey," she would say later, "I trusted him—the kid could count."

A day or two later the junta collapsed. Cokie was headed home in a cab when the news broke and she described the scene: "All of a sudden it was like Mardi Gras and New Year's Eve all at once. In all the cars, people honked their horns, and on the street, everyone was shouting and jumping up and down. Just then the radio in the cab announced the junta had fallen. I hopped out right at the Presidential Palace, where the civilian leaders were meeting, and turned on my tape recorder to capture all the sounds. Flower stalls lined one whole side of the building. I ran into one stall and commandeered the guy's telephone. Without so much as a by-your-leave, I took the phone apart and stuck these little alligator clips [the "thingamajig" she'd mentioned in a letter] into the receiver, which is the way you filed from a tape recorder in those years, and produced a spot. The flower-stall owner was screaming at me, convinced I was with the CIA, taking his phone apart. I calmed him down and bought some flowers. It was an incredibly exciting moment." That night, CBS called Cokie's mother and asked for her picture. Lindy was alarmed, but they reassured her: it was the biggest story in the world, Cokie's radio spot was the only report they had, so they were using it to lead the evening news on TV that night and wanted to post her photo while the audio was running. I was working from a British military base in Cyprus and couldn't get a phone line to call home, so I didn't know any of this. When I finally boarded a British military plane to London a week later, and then took a commercial flight back to Athens, I walked through the door to find I was married to a veteran foreign correspondent. As Cokie wrote to my parents: "The past week has given me undeniable credentials as a newswoman and I was at a stage where I very much needed that."

My bosses knew I was married to an extraordinary woman, who wanted to share the adventures I was having, so we forged a backdoor deal: the *Times* would pay for Cokie to travel with me on occasional reporting trips. When we landed in Italy right before a big election, she called CBS to say she was there and ready to work. "Thank goodness," they said. "Our radio reporter in Rome has just been taken to the hospital." She wound up covering the whole election and scooping me regularly, because her radio reports often aired before my stories were published. CBS realized her talent and she wrote to Cinda that the TV folks "asked me to do some film standups for them. They tell me they liked them and the guy is coming to town soon to talk about some work for them." The foreign editor did show up and said they were interested in hiring her as "their woman in Europe." She recalled her reaction: "There was no way on earth I could do that. Steve was away all the time. I'd be away all the time. Talk about unfair to your children! But it was fine to say no to that. It was flattering but it would have been wrong." Flattering, yes, but also frustrating. To Cinda she confessed: "They hired someone else to do it and now I resent it. I know it's ridiculous and I don't really regret any of the choices I've made but it would be nice to be able to do everything."

Still, after a democratic government was installed in Athens, and the news died down, Cokie grew restless, and the training she'd gotten from our "one-man journalism school" back in California kicked in. We did several travel pieces together and a long article for the *New York Times* Sunday magazine on a fascinating archeological dig on the island of Santorini. It was a Bronze Age site that had been buried in volcanic ash since about 1200 BC, and we spent one morning touring the excavation with the son of the shepherd who had discovered it years before. Then we ate a late lunch at a small seaside taverna nearby. The owner grilled some fish he'd caught that morning, picked a salad from his garden, and served the meal with a chilled bottle of local wine at a small table placed on the pebbly beach. We turned to each other and said, "We're on assignment! We're actually getting paid to be here!" It might have been the single best moment of our years abroad. Cokie's discontents were not our best moments, however, so she decided to start writing articles on her own, without my help, mainly for the Catholic magazine *Commonweal*. Just as we were leaving Athens and returning to Washington she wrote a story for the *Atlantic* based on a trip we'd taken to Istanbul. She'd noticed a sign outside a travel office in our hotel that read: EUROPE-ASIA HALF DAY TOUR. Istanbul is divided by the Bosphorus strait, which literally separates the two continents, and her article on the country's split personality was featured in the magazine's issue that was published just as we arrived home in the fall of 1977. Still, Cokie was dreading the prospect of looking for a job. "I'd done that before," she wrote. "It's horrible. I didn't want to do any of it. I didn't know what it was going to be like to be a grown-up here, raising children here, all of that. It was going back to my childhood in a way. I didn't know how any of that was going to work out and I didn't much want to learn."

Despite those fears, Cokie had no real choice: she needed to work to stay happy, and we needed a second salary to afford Washington. "Steven says now that the day my role shifted was the day I went to work at NPR," she said. "I would mark it a few weeks earlier than that—somewhere in the period after we got back to Washington and I realized necessity dictated that I had to have a full-time, well-paying job." The journalistic gods that had placed her in Athens when the military government collapsed, and turned her into a foreign correspondent, smiled once again. On my first day back in the Washington bureau, I was given a desk, looked around, and saw a young woman I didn't recognize. She said her name was Judy Miller and she used to work at National Public Radio. And I said, what's that? NPR had been on the air for six years but we'd been in Europe for the last four, and I'd never heard of it. When Judy described it, I instinctively said, "That's the perfect place for my wife to work. She's crying herself to sleep every night. What do I do?" And Judy said, call Nina Totenberg—then and now the Supreme Court reporter for NPR, who became one of Cokie's closest friends. I called Nina and she told me to get her Cokie's résumé immediately, which I delivered the next day, meeting her on the sidewalk outside the NPR studios. It was the first time I ever saw the old girls' network in action, with women helping one another in the way men had always done. At that memorable moment Cokie was thirty-three and had never worked a day as a full-time journalist. Nina immediately told Linda Wertheimer, who remembered Cokie from Wellesley, and started lobbying Jim Russell, then the news director. She also alerted Robert Siegel, who worked as an editor under Russell, and he had just read her piece in the *Atlantic*. "I had been very impressed with her article from Turkey," he recalled. "She was insightful. She wrote well. She was a good storyteller. She was the kind of person people would open up to. She struck me as a very good fit for NPR." Not everyone agreed, however, starting with Jim Russell. "I just felt that Cokie was not a journalist," he says now. "She came from a very strong and historic political family. Undoubtedly, she knew politics, having been weaned on it, but my feeling was that we were looking for someone who was a journalist and I didn't want to see us contaminate our purity. I said in a very simple fashion, this person is not a journalist. This person is a political animal. I was very monolithic in my view, and since that date I've always felt really silly."

Russell reluctantly agreed to take Cokie on as a temporary employee, but getting her hired full-time required more effort. Frank Mankiewicz, then the president of NPR, was slow to come around. "At one point he tells me he didn't want to hear anybody on the network named Cokie or Muffy or Buffy or anything like that," recalls Siegel. "He didn't like her name, he thought it was a preppy name and he didn't like that idea. He had hopes for a grittier network than perhaps NPR ever became. But that's clear in my mind, I found it very frustrating." Her full name was Mary Martha Corinne Morrison Claiborne Boggs Roberts—her nickname came from her brother, Tommy, who couldn't pronounce "Corinne"—and after Mankiewicz voiced his objections to Cokie, she devilishly signed off one evening with all seven of her names. At that point, Mankiewicz told the *Washington Post*, "I surrendered." But in the end her distinctive name served her very well. She was the only one. And when our grandchildren were born, and folks would ask what her "grandmother name" would be, she'd answer tartly: "Cokie. Don't you think one cutesy nickname is enough?"

Another problem was her voice. "She didn't have a velvety female voice, she didn't sound like a classic radio reporter, so in that sense she was not an instantly natural fit," recalls Siegel. To make matters worse, during one job interview with NPR executives she was suffering severely from allergies. "It was one of the worst showings of oneself in a job interview that you can imagine," says Siegel. "This was the pollen season and she was effectively in tears from an allergic reaction." What finally made the difference were her female allies Nina and Linda, who would not give up. Robert Krulwich, who shared editing duties with Siegel, remembers that quite clearly: "I mean, it was very definitely pressure. They were for her and wanted to recruit her and were not going to back down and they were not going to give up. They wanted her included because they loved her basically, they really loved her, they were crazy about her." When I asked Nina if sisterly solidarity had moved her to advocate for Cokie, she answered sharply: "Oh, absolutely. I wouldn't have done that for a man. No way." Cokie in turn embraced her new friends, telling the *New York Times*: "When I came in for an interview Linda and Nina were there, greeting me and encouraging me. And it just made all the difference in the world. NPR was a place I wanted to work because they were there."

Cokie's upset with our move back home did not end right away. "Nina got me in the door, but NPR didn't hire me," she recalled. "For a while I was on a weekly retainer. None of it was certain. In fact, even though I was filing stories almost daily, I wasn't hired for a long time. Steve's sister got married in October, and when we flew up to Boston, I cried the whole way. I couldn't see how any of this was going to get resolved. Nobody was hiring me, we couldn't afford to live anywhere, I felt like I was a child in my mother's house. It was all a mess, though I loved the work itself." It all did get resolved, partly because some of the men at NPR were also a bit "crazy" about Cokie. Krulwich kept talking about the "glow" she emitted and he recalled first meeting her years before, in the summer of 1968, at LaGuardia Airport in New York: "She was very beautiful and very pregnant, like eight months kind of pregnant. And I just remember thinking, wow, what a cool looking woman. And how lucky you were." Siegel had first heard about her from a journalism school classmate: "I remember him talking about the beautiful Cokie Boggs, maybe she was Cokie Roberts by that time, but she made a strong impression on people in a variety of ways."

Nina and Linda had so much clout because NPR, from its founding in 1971, featured women far more prominently than other broadcast networks. The *New York Times* Sunday magazine eventually celebrated the trio in a feature article that called them "the Three Musketeers: gutsy, witty, informed reporters who break stories from inside the Washington political machine." As a result, the *Times* concluded, "A new kind of female punditry was born." That public profile took years to develop, but from the very beginning "the Three Musketeers" formed an enduring alliance. Cokie, recalls Siegel, "became very close to Linda and Nina straightaway. That happened remarkably quickly." They went by other names as well—the Troika, and eventually the Founding Mothers—but their affection for each other never wavered, even as life took them in different directions. More than forty years after I handed Nina Cokie's résumé on that street corner in Washington, the three women and their husbands would often spend Saturday nights together, taking in a movie and eating at our favorite Italian restaurant. "It really did feel like the three Musketeers, it really did," says Nina. "You always knew that there were two other women that had your back always. And it continued throughout our lives, as you well know." In fact, public fascination with the "Founding Mothers" grew so great that *Parade* magazine once did a feature on their husbands. Nina at the time was married to a former senator, Floyd Haskell, and Linda's spouse, Fred, ran Common Cause, the public interest lobbying group. We joked with each other about being "the hidden husbands" of NPR.

Early on, the Musketeers moved their desks together in one corner of the NPR offices and appropriated an ugly old couch no one else wanted. Men sometimes derided their workspace as "the fallopian jungle," but to other women at NPR it was a refuge. "We had the couch there, in that space, no man ever came over there to lie down, I guarantee you. Only women came to lie down, or to talk out their problems," recalls Nina. Linda adds that "there were a lot of guys" who came to realize "these women were not without power. Don't cross us. You have to be careful if you're in the fallopian jungle, they'll jump you." To this day Robert Krulwich seems somewhat in awe of his female colleagues: "I thought it was like, wow, these women are really in it deep, and fiercely. They weren't afraid to announce that what they wanted was what they were going to get. They weren't afraid to bark, they weren't afraid to say, they weren't afraid to announce, they weren't afraid to tell. And that was new in the world." When I asked where that ferocity came from, he answered: "I'm not sure. It was kind of a stirring in the air. Nina was unabashed, Cokie was unabashed, Linda was unabashed. And it felt different. I was 25 or 26, so I didn't have much experience in the world at all, but I remember thinking, Hmm, I wonder if my dad ever had to deal with anything like this." Cokie writes about another tradition the three friends created: "One day, an editor at National Public Radio was flabbergasted when three of his reporters told him that if he wanted to reach us, we'd be in my kitchen. Steve's garden was in bounteous bloom and we had declared 'canning day,' where we bottled and pickled and froze all the produce, trading recipes and stories as we went along."

Whatever power the Founding Mothers acquired, they always used it to help others, particularly other women, not just themselves. Nina recalls: "That ugly old couch that we claimed and put there, I guess you could call it a place for psychotherapy when necessary. It was the place that women came when they had complaints about what was happening to them elsewhere in the building. When they were at their wits' end, they would come and say, so-and-so is embarrassing me with comments or kissing me on the cheek a little too much too often or hugging me. And we would go to the person and say, this is not really appropriate. It's embarrassing her. We wouldn't say the kinds of things you would say today, but we'd say it's embarrassing, or you need to back off a little bit."

One way that Cokie used her growing influence within NPR was during union negotiations. "She was always the voice of people with less power and the voice of what's right," says Nina. "I remember one day many years ago when we were in negotiations with NPR management over a labor contract. Management didn't want to extend health coverage to one group, and we were at an impasse. Then Cokie, who was working on a piece of embroidery, looked up at the management team and said, 'You know the position you're taking isn't immoral; it's simply amoral.' The room got very quiet, and soon, the impasse was over." Occasionally she got so angry that she'd lose her temper in those meetings.

The *Washington Post* quoted her telling NPR executives, "We're exhausted . . . we're tired of being this underpaid, we're tired of working in a filthy, dirty disgusting building . . . and we don't see how we can continue doing it." Her remarks "were met with applause," reports the *Post*, which then quotes Neal Conan, a longtime NPR fixture, about how the union would rely on Cokie when negotiations reached a critical point: "Tough? Are you kidding? You schedule the moments when you wheel in the big guns, and Cokie's the biggest gun of all. She's absolutely fearless."

At first the conflict Russell talked about, her membership in a prominent Democratic family, dissuaded her from covering politics. After all, her mother was by then a member of Congress, and as a young mom herself she was drawn to stories about education and social welfare policies. But Cokie could not escape her destiny. She had literally grown up in the Capitol, and that's where she belonged. Her father was first elected to Congress in 1940, three years before she was born, and she recalled for the *Washington Post* a moment when she was watching on TV some speech on the House floor. The camera operator had taken "an artsy shot from down low—the vantage point from which a very young person might view an ornate chamber filled with important men." The unusual camera angle jarred her memory. "It was knee-height," she recalled. "I was seeing myself. In the chamber. A little girl. Children always go in for the swearing-in . . . Swearing-in day is always my favorite day. It's in early January. I can't stand to miss it." She was probably wearing "Christmas velvet . . . white stockings and Mary Janes," she told the *Post*.

"And probably white gloves. I'm there with Daddy." It was January of 1949, she thinks, and the reporter asks how old she was. "Five," Cokie answers. "I would have just turned five." To another interviewer she recalled, "I had my seventh birthday in the Speaker's dining room. There was only one Senate office building, so all the towels said SOB, and there was a little rattan car that ran back and forth between it and the Capitol. There were times, when I was quite small, that my mother would just sort of park me on there and the poor guy running the tram was my babysitter, but they didn't seem to mind."

Her breakthrough came in the spring of 1978, almost thirty years after she had watched her father's swearing-in on the House floor. NPR was covering the Senate debate on the Panama Canal Treaty, the first live radio broadcast ever allowed from that chamber. Linda was the primary anchor, but Cokie filled in for her regularly, and Siegel recalls, "It became pretty evident, at least to me early on, that she was really talented and really smart. She was the backup to the main anchor but she really sounded terrific, she was awfully good at it." The shift in her assignment was not immediate, but it was probably inevitable. "Everybody understood she knew more than anybody else, had more contacts than anybody else, knew every parliamentary trick of the trade," says Nina. "So it was gradual, but it eventually happened that she started covering the Hill."

This would be like Michael Jordan's daughter covering basketball or Neil Armstrong's son writing about the space program. George Will, her Sunday-morning partner on ABC for years, put it this way: "If you don't like the game of politics, I don't see how you write about it well. It's as though someone said, I'm going to be a baseball writer, and I really don't like baseball. She liked the game of politics. She understood that in some ways it is a game, which is not a pejorative and not a diminishing and not a disparaging term. It's hard to connect cheerfulness and partisanship these days. She did it in her career and in her life."

Cokie's love for the US Capitol was boundless. As a child, she'd give tours for her father's visiting constituents. The only room in the entire building named for a woman honors her mother. The first female Speaker, Nancy Pelosi, asked to give a eulogy at her funeral. Yet she could still grow misty-eyed, viewing the dome, lit up late at night, as we left for home after covering an evening debate. Many reporters followed her around the Capitol over the years, and here's a typical report from the *Boston Globe* in 1981: "She knows all the committee doorkeepers, all the chauffeurs, all the people who work in the Hill restaurants, and never mind that one who used to call her 'baby' when she was a toddler did a double take the other day and said, 'I mean "Miz Baby."'" But it's not true, she declares, that House Speaker Tip O'Neill was once her babysitter. 'He just says that as a joke,' she says." But it was true, Cokie recalled for the *New York Times*, that "Tip O'Neill always said to me, 'I give you'se girls from NPR first shot at everything.'"

Because of her upbringing, Cokie always viewed politicians with more respect, and less cynicism, than her fellow reporters, and sources like O'Neill sensed that. "I do think I am more concerned about their privacy," she told *Fresh Air* on NPR, "but I also just see them much more as human beings, as people with all the flaws and foibles and families of a human being." And to the *Boston Globe* she admitted to having "a much more positive attitude about politics and politicians than most reporters. They are not a bunch of crooks. They have good homes and some rowdy children. I was one of them." The respect she felt was distinctly nonpartisan, and she stressed the importance of that influence to the *Washington Post*: "Growing up here in the '50s, a lot of the kids in school were political kids. The families moved here then, so we all knew each other across party lines and were friends. I mean, one of my best friends growing up, and still, is Libby Miller, whose father was a conservative Republican from Upstate New York who ran as Barry Goldwater's running mate. You know, I would go to her house and play board games. Now it's pretty hard to demonize someone whose child is playing Clue in the basement, right? Those sets of relationships—just normal relationships—really did make a difference."

One story illustrates Cokie's point perfectly. In 2006, she got a call from Susan Ford, daughter of President Gerald Ford and his wife, Betty. Mrs. Ford was planning her funeral and wanted Cokie to deliver one of the eulogies. "Mother wants you to talk about the way things used to be," Susan said. Cokie later explained what Susan meant: "A time in Washington when Democrats and Republicans used to be friends, when their families were all friends. The main message she wanted me to say is when you're friends, government works." Cokie often said that in today's Washington, it's impossible to imagine the wife of a Republican president asking the daughter of a Democratic congressman to deliver the eulogy at her funeral. Krulwich sums up Cokie's view of politics well: "Cokie was a believer at a time when everybody else was angry and disappointed and cynical."

Still, it was no secret Cokie came from a strongly Democratic family, and she had to work hard on the Hill to demonstrate her fairness as a reporter. The *Post* wrote: "She says she is aware that there has been some talk through the years about the propriety of her connections. What she's done, she says, is not pay attention. What she's done, she says, is to try and play it straight, walk the wire neatly, let the work speak for itself." And her work did speak for itself. Neal Conan of NPR told the *Post*: "One of the great tests of an appearance of a conflict is: does it raise questions in the minds of your audience? Well, our audience is not shy, let me tell you. We hear from everybody. I've never heard it raised once." *Lear's* wrote in 1993, right after Bill Clinton's election: "Roberts seems resolutely apolitical—as apt to deflate liberal dogma as conservative cant. That neutral stance has both surprised and aggravated people in the course of Roberts' career: During the presidential campaign Clinton people kept whining to Lindy Boggs, 'Why is Cokie so hard on us?' And in the progressive atmosphere of NPR, notes one colleague, 'Roberts' nonpartisanship wasn't an appreciated quality. She looked at everything as an open question, and there were those who distrusted her.'" I can say confidently that Cokie would have regarded that distrust as a compliment. She seldom if ever let her private feelings color her public judgment and was one of the few Washington reporters who consistently predicted Donald Trump's victory in 2016.

Cokie and I had a clear agreement that we would not write about her mother, which was really unfair to Lindy, since she hardly ever appeared in the *Times* or on NPR. And Lindy in turn did not play favorites with us. "She's the soul of discretion," Cokie cracked to one reporter, "the heck with that." But the mother-daughter bond was unbreakable. Their laughs were identical—people couldn't tell them apart—and so were their singing voices. At a moment's notice, they could launch into perfect harmony. Even if Lindy would not leak us stories, Cokie would always seek her out during lulls in congressional business. Often they would meet in the Speaker's lobby, just off the House floor, and as Cokie noted, "We sit down and put our feet up. It always makes members very nervous, wondering what we're talking about."

Even if she couldn't interview her mother, the sponsor of critical legislation guaranteeing equal credit for women, Cokie took a special interest in the other women serving in Congress and the issues they promoted, including more funding for breast cancer research, long before she was diagnosed with the disease herself. She described to students at the University of Southern California in 2015 how she covered debates over budget bills: "The negotiators would come out and my male colleagues would say, is the MX missile still in the bill? And I would say, is coverage for mammograms still in the bill? Now how many more people do you think are affected by coverage for mammograms than by

MX missiles? I still wrote about the MX missiles, but I asked about something that others weren't asking about."

"What happens to all women elected to Congress—including much to their amazement, women who are extremely conservative—is that they find they are the advocates for women and children all over the country," she told one interviewer, and in a sense she was also describing herself. Writing about issues affecting women and children helped push her toward the advocacy work she did later in her life, but her interest had always been there, deeply rooted in her fierce embrace of women's customary roles.

Another issue she felt deeply about was the mistreatment of women by male politicians. She later tangled on television with several male malefactors, from Bill Clinton to John Tower, but the sisterly support she received at NPR encouraged her to apply a female perspective to her reporting, and one example was coverage of political campaigns. "For years and years and years, it was all guys and they'd go rollicking off covering campaigns and having a wonderful time," she once asserted. "And nobody would ever report what was really going on because they'd all get in trouble with their bosses and their wives. So then women started showing up on the campaign trail and we actually thought that it was significant how a candidate treated women. So we would report on it. And the first big example of that was Gary Hart [the senator from Colorado whose bid for the Democratic nomination in 1988 was derailed by stories of his extramarital adventures]. But the fact is, we did not think that that was personal. If you're running for president, the way you treat women and your attitudes toward women is political. So we started reporting on it and we did change the way that candidates were assessed." In later years she reflected, "It's not an accident that Megyn Kelly is the person who asked Donald Trump about his statements about women, and it's not an accident that he went after her the way he did. The whole discussion about male treatment of women is something that we find relevant. And so I think it's very important to have that viewpoint reflected in the newsroom."

Cokie was ambitious and competitive, but she was always a generous colleague, even with rivals, willing to share her knowledge and insights about Congress and the Capitol. Bob Franken of CNN told the *Post*, "She's a tough adversary. She sets the standard really. At the same time she's a dear friend. You can be brutal during the day, fighting for the story, but then it's over. Regrettably, more often than not, she's the brutalizer, I'm the brutalizee."

As always Cokie was particularly kind to other women, and after she died, *Washington Post* columnist Karen Tumulty remembered their days working together: "When I was starting out as a reporter on Capitol Hill, we would often have lunch together at a table set aside for the press in the House restaurant. I loved to hear her talk. She knew all the backstories of Washington, had a deep understanding of its institutions and was generous in sharing her insights with those of us still trying to figure out how the place worked. Somehow, she never became jaded or lost her ability to appreciate big things and small ones. Once, as we were trudging down the stairwell that leads from the lobby off the House Chamber, she paused and called my attention to the tiny cherub statues embedded in the cast-iron railings—something I had passed hundreds of times and never noticed. 'Look at their little bottoms,' she said. 'Aren't they adorable?' I never walked that way again without thinking of Cokie. She won plenty of prizes for her work, and blazed a path for others, particularly women. But what distinguished her journalism was not sensational scoops, or the kind of thing that goes viral today and is gone tomorrow. It was consistency and common sense."

Her listeners understood that. After her death I heard from countless people, talking about how she had inspired them, and one of those notes came from a former student, Sabi Chawla, the daughter of an immigrant cabdriver from India who now lives in London: "It was my dad who broke the news to me about Cokie. He heard about it on the radio and from his DC cab he texted me here in London to say, 'I'm sorry about your Cokie.' Though we never met her, she was personal to my family. She was the role model my mom used to motivate me. She would see her on TV and say, 'You can be like Cokie if you're smart and strong.'" Smart and strong and true to yourself. As she once put it, "I know exactly who I am and I'm comfortable with that."

She did know who she was—a wife and mother, a sister and daughter, a neighbor and friend, a real person with a real dog who did her own grocery shopping at the local Safeway. As she got more famous, people would occasionally approach her in the store and wonder why she was there, loading up her cart like everyone else. She always found those encounters amusing, and would say later that she was tempted to tell those fans, "Who else is going to do my shopping? Would you like to do it for me?" One incident that humanized her for NPR audiences involved Abner the basset hound, the same creature who had pooped all over our kitchen floor one night after we'd been talking about a new book on CNN. Abner was eager to be on the radio, and one Monday morning, when Cokie was doing her regular broadcast from home, he started barking right in the middle of her segment. She wasn't sure that anyone could hear the rascal, but they could—clearly—and deluged NPR with queries. So the next morning she went back on the air with Bob Edwards, the host of *Morning Edition*, and he said, "OK, 'fess up, Cokie." It's true, she replied, I broadcast from home, "in my very discreet nightie," and Abner finally made it onto the air after years of trying. That darn dog became a folk hero to NPR listeners, and for years afterward, folks would come up to us and ask, "How's Abner?" At one point a photo history of NPR was published, and it contained two photos of Cokie—and three of Abner.

Cokie never lost her affection for radio, and continued her connection with NPR for the rest of her life. "She was really devoted to NPR. Even after she worked principally for ABC and only partly for us, she did fundraiser after fundraiser, speech after speech for every station," recalls Nina. "She really cared about this network desperately. She thought it was an essential part of a democratic system." For many years she continued her Monday morning chats and then created a highly popular feature, "Ask Cokie," which drew heavily on her understanding of history. "I love it," she told the *Post* about her radio career. "It's work I can only do there. Because the medium of radio is just different. Your writing is much more a part of the story. What you are aiming for in radio is for people to imagine the picture."

But radio was simply too small a stage to contain her enormous talent and expanding reputation. She had started to do some occasional TV in the late '70s, and a producer from PBS, Linda Winslow, was looking for someone to help host a new show she was creating about Congress. She saw Cokie interviewed by the commentator Bill Moyers and immediately sensed what Sophie Altman, and those CBS producers who had wanted her to be their "woman in Europe," had already discovered. "I just was struck by this particular woman, her personality just came shooting through the television screen and she just had this combination of knowledge and of relatability," Winslow says. "You could easily see having a cup of tea with her, and exchanging good gossip. I just thought she was made for TV." I asked if she knew anything about Cokie's family connections to Congress and Linda gave a revealing answer: "No, none whatsoever. I had no idea how she knew so much. I just figured she was covering the Hill and she did her homework and really spent a lot of time with these people, so she got to know them very well."

When Winslow approached NPR about using Cokie for the new show, called *The Lawmakers*, she was told that the network had two congressional correspondents, and how about using them both? So that's what happened—Cokie and Linda Wertheimer teamed with Paul Duke, the chief anchor at PBS, on a weekly broadcast that lasted for the next few seasons. The only problem was that the two women often shopped together and would show up on the set wearing the same-colored blouse. So on Thursdays, show day, they had to start consulting in the morning about what they were wearing. After *The Lawmakers* ended, PBS started *NewsHour*, which still exists with Judy Woodruff as host. As Winslow recalled, the producer of *NewsHour*, Les Crystal, "had seen *The Lawmakers* and he had seen Cokie on it and he thought the same thing I thought. He thought she was a natural, and so he wanted her to be the congressional correspondent. But she, wisely, didn't want to be a full-timer, she wanted to keep her NPR job." So she worked for *NewsHour* part-time, but it was not a happy match. "She said, well, this isn't fun," says Winslow. The show was like an "all-boys school," very different from NPR, where women had attained so much influence, and Cokie felt it responded too slowly to breaking news. In private moments she would say the show's slogan should be "Yesterday's News Tomorrow." But one event did showcase her talents: PBS's coverage of congressional hearings into the Iran-Contra Affair during the end of the Reagan presidency. She joined an all-female cast, which included Woodruff and commentator Elizabeth Drew, and as one report noted, "Praise for their coverage has poured in from a wide range of viewers—including a spectrum of columnists from William F. Buckley Jr. to Carl Bernstein—and, most enthusiastically, from feminists. 'Woodruff, Drew, and Roberts are doing as much for the women's movement as they are doing for the rest of America,' says Kate Rand Lloyd, editor at large of *Working Woman* magazine." The *San Francisco Chronicle* reported that "Roberts recalled the mail she got from viewers of the Iran-Contra hearings who 'never had the experience before of seeing a program where all the authorities were female.' And the impact of the three PBS women? 'Perhaps it's like electing your first Catholic president,' Roberts said. 'Once you've done something the first time it becomes easier for everybody who comes along next.'"

When Cokie's old friend from Los Angeles days, Tom Brokaw, brought up the idea of her moving to NBC, she was interested. But Brokaw's boss at the time, Tom Pettit, advanced the same concerns that had once bothered Jim Russell at NPR years before. "I really wanted to hire her and Tom wouldn't do it, because he said 'she's too political for us,' and I was furious about that," Brokaw told me. "I said, 'Tom, it's crazy, I mean she's an independent woman. It's unfair for her to be judged by what other members of her family do.' And he said, 'I don't care.' I think he was throwing his weight around, quite honestly, and I was pissed off. And it was very hard for me to go to Cokie and say, 'I'm sorry, it's not going to work.' And she said, 'I can't believe that,' and I said, 'Neither can I, Cokie. But go do well elsewhere.' And obviously she did. It was a big miss for us."

CHAPTER FOUR

Journalist, in Full Flower

"I remember thinking, the varsity had arrived."

Yes, it was a very "big miss" for NBC, and when ABC came calling Cokie was ready to listen. For most of the 1980s that network's Sunday-morning show, *This Week*, was number one in the ratings, but it featured three aging white guys—David

Brinkley, George Will, and Sam Donaldson—and pressures were growing to make the cast more diverse. Several female journalists had been appearing occasionally on the roundtable at the end of the program, but none of them excited Roone Arledge, then head of the network's news division. Bob Murphy, a senior executive at ABC, recalled: "Roone wanted a female voice on the roundtable. There were a group of women who were very smart, very talented, but they were not distinguished in a way that Roone was looking for. They were black-and-white and he was looking for somebody that popped out in living color." And the three dominant males weren't thrilled with the female panelists either. "There were some women, but they never really were the equal of the men," notes Murphy. "And the men didn't treat them as equals."

Folks at ABC knew of Cokie from her work at NPR and PBS, and she was brought in for a onetime trial to join the roundtable on October 25, 1987. I remember that morning well. I was watching at home, and even though I had been married to Cokie for more than twenty-one years at that point, I found myself gasping—at those smarts, that smile, that laugh, those eyes, those blazing blue eyes. Boy, did she pop out "in living color." Marc Burstein, then an assistant producer on the show, remembers, "It was a different time, when women went on roundtables, even on Sunday public affairs shows, they weren't often speaking about politics, and certainly not as knowledgeably as Cokie did. And she immediately commanded the respect of George and David and Sam, which was no easy task in of itself. She talked with a confidence and an air of authority that you just knew she wasn't making it up. It was intrinsically in her bones. And Roone liked celebrities, liked stars, and Cokie had a star quality about her even then." Murphy recalls the reaction among the network's brass: "Well, that was good, let's have her back again. And then another week, another week, and then all of a sudden, everybody claimed that they discovered her and they knew all along how great she was going to be. Cokie would be the first one to point that out and be amused by the whole thing." Dorrance Smith, then the producer of *This Week*, put it this way: "She fit in, in ways that others didn't. It became her chair. She earned it."

Still, recognition came slowly. "When I first started the Brinkley show, I think I was regarded as the token girl, and they resented me," Cokie told *Lear's*. "It's difficult for a woman in those circumstances. If you interrupt too much and are too aggressive and ready to get in there, you come across as a bitchy shrill witch. And if you don't talk enough and are polite and wait, then you come across as a wallflower with nothing to say." TV was like one of those stuffy old men's clubs, which only allowed women in through a side door, if at all. To illustrate the obstacles she faced in those early days, Cokie often told the story about one Sunday morning, when the cast was gathering before the show, having breakfast and trading stories. As usual, the male regulars were ignoring her, and their conversation turned to New Orleans. One of them mentioned that he'd been to a beautiful historic home in the French Quarter, owned by Lindy Boggs, then a member of Congress. Cokie, to her astonishment, realized the men didn't know about her relationship. "Guys," she recalled breaking in, "that's my mother!"

The guys dispute that story, but they agree that she "earned" her spot, and their respect. "I remember thinking, the varsity had arrived," says George Will. "Cokie liked the camera and the camera liked her. She came through it into your living room, completely at ease, and she came trailing clouds of Washington authenticity. That gave her a kind of sureness and confidence and ease around the passing swirl of things. She was largely immune to the abiding failure of Washington journalism, which is to think that everything's as momentous as it feels at the moment." The producers kept inviting her back because they knew their audience and what they wanted, especially on Sunday morning. As Will puts it: "They didn't tune in to *This Week* to get a variety of personalities. They wanted something familiar. And a show like that is a little like a jazz quartet or a basketball team. Just a lot of flow and improvisation and knowing where everyone was going."

Cokie's relationship with Brinkley was also critical. He was then sixty-seven, a pioneer in broadcast journalism who had cohosted *The Huntley-Brinkley Report* on NBC for many years. He could be cranky and cantankerous, but he was also a fellow Southerner, a native of North Carolina, and Cokie just charmed her way into his good graces. She provided, says Dorrance Smith, "a comfort zone for him. I think her sense of humor and his sense of humor were a lot alike and they made each other laugh." Brinkley also came to respect her deeply as a professional broadcaster.

"Cokie knows more about Congress than any single member knows, and ten times more than I ever did," Brinkley told *Lear's*. And besides, "she has never been intimidated by being on the air with three smart alecks."

By the next year, ABC offered her a contract to become a regular contributor to the network. Not only was she a rising star, but a group of women at ABC were pressuring their bosses to elevate females into more prominent roles. Carole Simpson says that making Cokie a permanent member of the Sunday roundtable was one of their goals. "She had proven herself on the show and we had a long list of grievances with ABC about women," said Simpson, who later became the anchor of the network's weekend news.

Cokie was "very nervous about network television," she once explained, because she disliked doing short, scripted stories and she worried about ageism against women: "Obviously how you look is important and how a woman looks is more important than how a man looks. And there is a serious question about how long they'll let a bunch of women who are getting wrinkled and a little thicker around the midriff, stay on the air." That anxiety showed itself when Cokie first met with Amy Entelis, then the ABC executive in charge of hiring new talent. "I remember Cokie coming in with a little bit of an attitude, of like what would you do with me? Why would you want me?" Entelis tells me. "She was not super eager actually, a little dubious about whatever it was we might have in our mind. My impression from that meeting was that she had it exactly right in her life and her career. She wasn't jumping up and down with glee that we wanted her to be part of ABC News." Eventually ABC alleviated her concerns by agreeing to a contract that also permitted her to continue working for NPR. "We were so determined to get her that we made this unusual arrangement that allowed her, in effect, to serve two masters," ABC's bureau chief at the time, George Watson, told the *Washington Post*.

There were many reasons for Cokie's success on the Sunday show, starting with the "clouds of authenticity" and "air of authority" that she naturally projected. And while many men found her appealing, what really set her apart was the way she connected with other women in the audience. Linda Winslow, who had hired Cokie for *The Lawmakers* on PBS, recalls the impact she made: "She would talk about the dynamic of the discussion on the Brinkley show, where the guys would talk to each other and she'd have to try to get a word in edgewise. But she always managed when she did to say something to elicit a wave of response from female viewers, including me. It would be like, yes, that's the point they're missing. There was always an edge to her stories that emphasized that it was the women who made change happen in many instances, the women who were in the background, the women who work without getting recognition. I remember in particular when the Pope came to Washington and she went around connecting with the nuns and getting their story, a much better story than anybody else got. And she did that on ABC quite a lot because I know friends of mine would comment that yes, I'm watching ABC more because when Cokie's on she always speaks up and says what I'm thinking." Jean Becker, who eventually became chief of staff to President George H. W. Bush, was a journalism student when Cokie joined the roundtable, and she recalls, "Women like Cokie made me feel that I could do anything I wanted to do. She gave us confidence. To see her go toe to toe with her male colleagues or her male interview subjects, it just made all the difference in the world."

Cokie was very aware that women were rooting for her, and she made this insightful comment to *TV Guide*: "You know, men come up to me on the street and say, 'We like your common sense on the Brinkley show.' But women say, 'We love the way you don't let them interrupt you, and that you hand it right back to them.' I get the feeling that the country is full of women who've never gotten a word in edgewise when men talk politics." As her role at ABC began to expand, she started subbing for Ted Koppel as the host of *Nightline*, and that show's producer, Tom Bettag, described her appeal in the *Washington Post*: "I think it has to do with reaching a certain maturity and wisdom. She is somehow extraordinarily comfortable with herself. There's an 'I-am-what-I-am' quality that comes across extremely well. I think a little of it is that she isn't a 28-year-old blonde, ironically. There's nothing in here that says, 'I want to cover my neck because my neck gives away my age.' And so all of it works."

Cokie liked to describe herself as "everywoman" or a "suburban housewife," and one TV critic called her "everybody's sensible and admired big sister." All true, but few suburban housewives were so good on TV, and while audiences loved what she said, they also loved how she said it. "Roberts provides her own irrepressible laugh track," wrote *Lear's*. "On the Brinkley show, the trademark chuckle often announces her presence before the camera finds her. 'There's some thinking that cackling on television is unattractive,' she says. 'But that's not what the viewers think. I hear that *a lot* from people. It's such a treat to hear you laugh.'" As *Lear's* put it, "However portentous the circumstances, she extends the tantalizing possibility that fun may break out."

Along with that laugh came the eye roll, a distinctly female gesture generally aimed at puncturing a particularly fatuous male comment. *Lear's* wrote about her eyeballs bulging "so wide that the startling blue irises are completely surrounded by white. They invite complicity as surely as the ironic lift of the brow and the slight curl of the lip." Other women got it, out in TV land but also sitting next to her in the studio. "I loved Cokie's eye roll," says Martha Raddatz, who regularly hosts the Sunday show on ABC that Cokie first joined in 1987. "If you were sitting with her on election night or an inaugural or a parade or whatever it was, through many administrations—that eye roll of Cokie's, you knew what she was really thinking. And let's face it, over these years, she was up against a lot of men on those panels. That never stopped Cokie Roberts, she was going to get her point in and it was always so compelling because it came with such a depth of knowledge."

Cokie's tolerance for male pomposity was pretty low, that's partly why so many women were tuning her in, and it led to some noteworthy confrontations on the air. Perhaps the most famous came in 1989, when President George H. W. Bush nominated a former senator, John Tower, as secretary of defense. Tower was well-known for his drinking habits, and when he came on the Sunday show he made a strange pledge to abstain from alcohol, but only if his nomination was confirmed by the Senate. Sam Donaldson then brought up rumors of "womanizing." Tower demanded a definition from Sam, who couldn't provide one. "And then," Cokie recalled, "basically because I'm sitting there in a skirt, he turns to me and says, 'Cokie, do you have a definition of the term?'" She shot back with eleven of the most memorable words she ever said on television: "I think most women know it when they see it, Senator." Donaldson recalls Tower's reaction: "I mean he was deflated. It was hard for John Tower who was diminutive to begin with to deflate, but physically you could almost feel it, deflating right in the chair." Cokie described the public reaction that followed: "People got mad. Senators who had not heard a word against Tower to that moment got mail saying, 'Why was he beating up on that woman? Why was he so rude to that woman?'" Tower was later rejected by the Senate, an exceptionally rare fate for any cabinet nominee, especially one who had served in that body for twenty-four years.

Then there was Ross Perot, the Texas businessman who ran for president as an independent in 1992. He was so enamored of Cokie that he once considered her as a potential running mate. But when she interviewed him on *Nightline*, and asked a series of tough questions, Perot went nuts. "The whole interview became just unbelievably testy, and it just got ruder and tenser and awful,"

Cokie recalled for the *New York Times*. "We just sat there thinking, 'Is he gonna get up and leave? Is he gonna throw the chair? Is he gonna strangle himself on his microphone?'" The next week he made this comment about female reporters: "They're all trying to prove their manhood."

Perot had it exactly wrong. Cokie was proving her womanhood, not her manhood. As Linda Winslow noted, one of her main motivations was to ask questions that other women wanted to know the answers to, and didn't hear from male interviewers. She was particularly tough on men like Tower, who she felt had used and abused women, but her scorn crossed party lines, and she could barely conceal her disdain for Bill Clinton. During the New Hampshire primary of 1992, when Clinton was fighting for his political life, she was moderating a debate among the Democratic contenders and asked him whether his reputation for infidelity would cripple his candidacy. We had many old friends working for the Clinton campaign and they were furious with her, but she never backed down, and never really warmed to Clinton either. During the Monica Lewinsky scandal that blighted Clinton's second term, his lawyer David Kendall came on the Sunday show and tried to justify the president's claim that oral sex did not contradict his famous statement that "I did not have sex with that woman, Miss Lewinsky." Cokie asked Kendall if his wife would accept Clinton's defense and definition, and Sam Donaldson, who was sitting right next to her, describes the lawyer's unhinged reaction: "Once again, here is a man who has no answer. The segment ended and David got up to leave and instead of walking toward the door, he was so rattled by the question that he almost walked into a standing lamp that was lighting the set. It was terrible, but that was Cokie at her best." Kendall didn't exactly agree and was so angry that he told the *Post*, "If dueling were still allowed, somebody would be dead." The public reaction was considerably more favorable, however. As Robin Sproul, then the ABC bureau chief, recalls, "So many women reacted so positively to her saying, 'Well, have you asked your wife about that?' She just spoke in a way like you'd speak to somebody in the grocery store."

Linda Douglass, who had a long career as a TV journalist, recalls how she came to respect Cokie's "unshakeable moral core." She was skeptical at first, and critical of Cokie's question to Clinton during the New Hampshire debate. "I had never run into any big journalist, an anchor level journalist, who was as judgmental about human flaws in a male politician as Cokie was," says Douglass. "I just thought, well, Cokie must have a level of rectitude that is unusual in politics and maybe one that is not representative of the way the public should feel." But over the years she changed her view. "I have never forgotten that Cokie was the one, in a really simple way, who made the case that you're not going to be a good leader if you don't have a strong moral core. It changed from something that I kind of chuckled at initially to something that really was a beacon for me in a lot of ways."

Tom Bettag, the *Nightline* producer, called Cokie "a bit of a scold," and that's true. Not only did she pass moral judgment on men she interviewed, like Tower and Clinton, the targets of her derision could include her colleagues and bosses. Robin Sproul, who became the Washington bureau chief and Cokie's close friend, was a pioneering female executive in a male-dominated business. "So to have another woman who you could talk to, that felt like a safe space," she told me. "And Cokie was really good at helping you see clearly what your own way was, and that you could probably outsmart those people because they were spending so much time in the bar or out with a girlfriend or on a golf course. If you just showed up to work and did your job, and did a really good job, it was probably a winning strategy." As for Cokie, says Sproul, those male bosses "were just a little bit afraid of her because they knew that when those piercing eyes looked at them, they could see there was judgment there. It was not 'all is forgiven.' It was like, 'I'll deal with you, know that I see you.' They saw in her eyes that she saw through them, and I think ultimately that was just fine and kept the respect level very high."

One male boss Cokie occasionally clashed with was Roone Arledge, who ran ABC News from 1977 to 1998 and died in 2002. He appreciated her on-air presence, that she "popped out in living color," and he supported the idea of making her a regular panelist on the Sunday show. "He liked the program and liked the chemistry and the seriousness and quite frankly, he liked the ratings," says Bob Murphy. But on a personal level, Cokie shared few if any values with Roone, who married three times and hobnobbed with New York's glitterati at his weekend house in the Hamptons. She had a life outside of her work, and she had no trouble turning the boss down on occasion. She wouldn't miss a child's birthday, or interrupt a family vacation, just to be on TV one more time. And she paid a price for that, says Tom Bettag: "Cokie was not one of Roone's favorites because she told him no. I think he had real enthusiasm for her talent, but I think Roone saw Cokie as a pain in the ass. Cokie does what Cokie wants to do and she won't listen half the time."

Then there was how Cokie looked. Television is a visual medium, and Larry Drumm, who did Cokie's makeup for many years, says that Arledge "was adamant" that the network's female talent "present a unified look" on the air. When I asked him to describe that look Larry replied: "Polished, well-educated, affluent, a very Upper East Side, professionally made-up, coiffed wealthy woman. And that went across the board for everybody pretty much except Cokie. Cokie had a natural beauty, I mean it just came through, and with a lot of makeup, Cokie would not look like Cokie, and would not be perceived as Cokie." When Larry would relay Roone's instructions to make her look more glamorous, Cokie would snap back: "Well I'm not in New York, and I'm my own person, and if they have an issue, they can call me directly." She had a very clear conviction that how she looked on TV had to fit with what she said. She wanted everything about her to convey "sensible"—her hair, her makeup, her clothes. "It's not that I don't appreciate make-up," Cokie told *Lear's* as she was approaching fifty. "I want to look like me, only better, not like someone else. I don't want to look like some glamorous twenty-two-year-old—I'm the mother of a glamorous twenty-two-year-old!" On NPR's *Fresh Air* she disputed the notion that she was some "prim" opponent of makeup. "Quite the contrary, I've been trying to get the makeup man to move in with me for years," she joked. "And I mean, I am delighted to look good, you know? Nothing makes me happier than looking like a better version of myself. But that's who I have to look like is myself, and so there's been a continuing fight over these long skirts that I wear, and I just cannot imagine trying to make an argument and make a forceful point against Sam tugging on my skirt, you know? It's one thing too many to think about."

How she looked became a bigger problem after she was first diagnosed with breast cancer in 2002, and chemotherapy caused her hair to fall out. She hated the idea of people treating her as "sick," and would have kept her illness private if at all possible. But she knew her fans would notice a change in her appearance, so she arranged for a trusted reporter at the *Washington Post* to disclose her condition. "I felt at first going on the air in a wig that I looked really goofy," she recalled. "And election night 2002, it was my best wig, it was the human hair wig, not the synthetic wig, and I thought it just looked awful." As her hair grew back, she was eventually able to ditch the wig. And as the years went by, she never tried to hide her age, never had a bit of cosmetic surgery, always wanted to look like herself "only better." But she was always keenly aware that "the jury's still out on how long a woman can be on TV."

After signing that contract with ABC in 1988, and moving her base of operations from radio to TV, Cokie steadily enlarged her role and her visibility. In June of 1993, just months before she turned fifty, the *Washington Post Magazine* mused about the strange course of her career, delayed for so many years by following me around the world. "She's a late bloomer on the infernal box," they wrote. "Somehow she's reached critical mass in cathode-ray consciousness at about the point when most women in the business can look forward to getting dumped." Cokie reacted with wry amusement, her usual stance on the subject of her unusual professional odyssey. "Yes, fresh-faced at 49," she cracked. "Thank God for the baby boomers."

In addition to her Sunday-morning gig, she was subbing regularly on *Nightline*, commenting on *Good Morning America*, reporting for the evening news, and analyzing live events like conventions, elections, and presidential speeches. She also appeared every Monday morning on NPR (yes, often in her nightgown). One of her specialties was the Catholic church, and she loved reporting from Rome, especially during the late '90s, when her mother was the American ambassador to the Vatican. When the new millennium began, and ABC covered the event for twenty-four hours as calendars flipped around the world, Cokie reported from the Holy City and interviewed Lindy. When a Jesuit, Jorge Mario Bergoglio, was unexpectedly chosen as the new Pope in 2013, she could barely contain her excitement. Her uncle Robbie had been a Jesuit; her brother, Tommy, and her son, Lee, had gone to Jesuit schools; and she blurted into the microphone, "You don't know what a big deal this is!" Or words to that effect. "That was just another example where Cokie was invaluable," notes Marc Burstein, who has produced ABC's live events for many years. "That's just something you loved about her, her exuberance when she had something that she believed was important to say. Sometimes I would actually have to say, 'Cokie, your mic wasn't open for half of what you said,' because she would catch the audio people off guard."

Cokie always saw herself as an advocate for women, and she used her visibility to highlight the issue of breast cancer long before she was diagnosed with the disease herself. A turning point came in 1991, when two of her friends died of breast cancer in the same week. As she told journalist Ali Rogin: "They were in adjoining rooms in the funeral home. The masses were staggered so everybody could go to both. And I just got mad. I wrote an op-ed for the *Washington Post* that was picked up around the country. At that point the funding for all of cancer and all of heart disease combined was less than the funding for AIDS. And of course I'm for AIDS funding but that was because of advocacy. I do remember doing *Nightline* one night when I was the anchor, and there was some new data out on breast cancer. I insisted on doing a whole show on it, and they basically treated me like I wasn't there, like I was just invisible. And everybody was just eye rolling. I remember saying to the executive producer, 'You know men really might care because they want somebody to fold their socks.' And of course, it turned out to be an incredibly well-watched show because it affects so many people." In 2005, three years after her own diagnosis, Cokie helped organize a panel of women from ABC to talk about their own experiences with breast cancer for a TV special. One of them, Amy Entelis, describes Cokie's role:

"She created a space for all of us to talk about scary things and our experiences and share them widely. That was just another of those things that Cokie did that went far beyond anything anybody had ever tried before."

While Cokie could be deadly serious about promoting women and their interests, she often employed her mischievous sense of humor to needle powerful men. In 1995, when Disney bought ABC, there was a grand event to celebrate the merger, and Cokie was assigned to interview Michael Eisner, then the boss at Disney. One question she asked him was, "What is Goofy?" referring to the popular cartoon character. As Cokie loved to tell the story, Eisner answered that Goofy was a dog. But then how was it, Cokie continued, that Goofy had a pet dog named Pluto? Did that make Pluto a dog's dog? Now Cokie was bending things a bit—Pluto was generally identified as Mickey Mouse's pet, but on occasion he *was* depicted as belonging to Goofy, and Eisner, Cokie crowed, was totally undone by her question. There are few people with the confidence, and the wit, to throw their new boss into a fit of public confusion.

Along with all the free speeches Cokie made for ABC and many other organizations she cared about, her career as a paid speaker was also taking off. I asked her longtime agent Beth Gargano why she was in such demand. "She listened, a lot of people don't do that," Beth replied. "Before she went to a lecture she needed to know what they were about and what they wanted her to talk about. She actually paid attention to the background we gave her on an actual audience. But then when she got there, she had that way of making you feel like you've been her best friend since childhood. It was just magic." One night, after a reception that followed her lecture, Cokie saw that plenty of food was left over and she told the meeting planner to pack it up and take it home. As Beth tells the story, the woman demurred, but Cokie insisted: "'Let's get some Saran Wrap and I'll pack it up for you. Didn't you say you had kids? They'll eat this!' And Cokie literally packed up the food and made sure it got in the woman's car. That was a story that really traveled around the industry, because the meeting planners were all women and they fell in love with her."

Fame brought with it a certain amount of scrutiny and criticism, and Cokie was not used to that. She had always been the good girl, the model child, and she was not happy when a *Washington Post* article about highly paid speech makers called her a "buckraker." Beth Gargano says, "I think they singled her out because she was a woman, I really do, and it got to her, it really got to her. She was so embarrassed by it because that was her nature, not to ever discuss money. It really disgusted her that she was out there in the forefront of that story."

One night she was doing a rushed piece for the evening news about Congress and there was not enough time for her to get to Capitol Hill before the broadcast, so a producer suggested she wear a coat in the studio and report in front of a photo. It was a small deception, but she and the producer were both reprimanded for it, and Robin Sproul remembers that episode as a "very tough time" for Cokie: "I was in her office as it came to a head and

Cokie was crying and I said to her, 'Oh my God, has nobody ever criticized you before?' And she said, 'No, not really, no, not like this. I don't do things to be criticized for.' We laughed about it later but it was really a shock to her system." The internet has created a toxic environment for many journalists, especially women, and I would encourage Cokie to ignore the vile things that people said about her on social media, but she would still take peeks occasionally and get offended. She once told David Letterman, "Nothing is worse than the computer mail. On the internet people are anonymous and they feel complete freedom to say any old dreadful thing. There really is something to be said for good manners. Now I have a form letter that says, 'Your mother would be ashamed of you.'"

That was the public Cokie, the one who asked the questions women wanted to hear, who held her own with those "smart aleck" men, who insisted that morality mattered in politics, and inspired a generation of young women to feel "that I could do anything I wanted to do." But some of the most significant contributions Cokie made during her thirty-two years at ABC were private not public, behind the scenes not in front of the cameras. David Westin, who ran ABC News for thirteen of those years, described her influence this way: "The thing that people may not appreciate is she busted the chops of the old guys above her who were not giving the proper opportunity to women. And she busted my chops, she would come after me. She'd come up to my office and really have at me about what was going on. She felt there was 'an old boys' club' and she was very, very assertive on behalf of women in the business. She made sure they were getting their proper due and proper respect, and frankly, that's the way she contributed as much as anything else."

One notorious example involved Martha Raddatz, now one of the network's leading lights. After she was hired from NPR in 1999, the star anchor Peter Jennings would not put her on *World News*, the network's premier show, for well over a year, notes Westin: "I'd beat up on them, and they refused to do it, and it enraged Cokie, enraged her. And she was right. It was really tough with a lot of anger and a lot of tears, but Cokie was on my case saying, 'This is ridiculous, you've got to stop this.' When she saw injustice, she was not shy, she spoke up and called it out for what it was." Raddatz recalls that period as "really tough and really discouraging" and she "almost left" the network. But with Cokie's encouragement, and support from other women in the bureau, she decided to outflank the men who were blocking her from *World News*, by working weekends and contributing to other shows. "If you were having a bad day, you could go down to Cokie's office, and you often felt guilty about that, because Cokie had a few bad days herself, but it was like I needed a quick little hit of Cokie to keep going," Raddatz remembers. Eventually Martha flourished and became the network's chief global affairs correspondent. Now she says, "I would not be here except for Cokie," and other women who helped her through the "really tough" times. "I mean, who has the courage to go and fight for what they thought was right, without fear of their own careers?

Cokie was the leader of that pack of women who want to do the right thing."

Another example of how Cokie used her leverage to help women was Donna Brazile, a Democratic strategist who started appearing as a panelist on *This Week* after Cokie broke the gender line and ABC actually invited more than one woman on the set at a time. Says Donna: "Cokie used to give me the eye and the eye would be, Donna, go ahead and say it. You're not gonna hurt anyone's feelings. You know it's the truth. So say it. And I always felt comfortable when I was surrounded by her, because she knew the politics better than most people on the set, whether it was George Will, Sam Donaldson or whatever the team was at the time. She also understood that I was quite intimidated to be in that circle, but Cokie pushed me to become something that I didn't think I could ever be, to use my voice to speak up and speak out, to tell that truth, to tell it with facts, not just emotion, whether it was on issues involving race or class or poverty. And she would always come behind me and she would say Donna's right. Or she would add to what I said, and let me go further. She looked after me, she made sure I had a seat at the table."

Lynn Sherr had known Cokie since college, and when they both found themselves covering politics for ABC they relied heavily on each other for moral support. "Cokie was never shy about saying sisterhood is powerful," says Lynn. "Cokie was never shy about saying, we really are in this together and we're stronger when we're together. And that was one of the truly remarkable things about her. I have worked with many women, in many circumstances, some of whom I couldn't care less about, and they couldn't care less about me. But there was never a moment I thought Cokie wouldn't have my back if I needed her and that we couldn't run to the ladies' room and have a good laugh about something that had just happened or a good cry. She just made it possible to relate in a way that was so wonderful and refreshing and exactly right for our time."

Cokie "busted the chops" of the network brass on behalf of any woman she felt was being mistreated, not just on-air personalities like Raddatz. Jackie Walker, a makeup artist and close friend, was complaining about an occasional guest on the Sunday show who would—to put it delicately—play with himself while in her makeup chair. But instead of barring the guest, management told Jackie they "would bring somebody else in" to work in her place when that guest was scheduled. Cokie was furious and said so. Her bosses, notes Jackie, "weren't going to stand up for me, but Cokie was going to stand up for me." Together they hit on a scheme. Jackie crafted a particularly short smock, "the pervert cape" as she called it, "that no longer covered the crotch" of the self-pleasuring panelist and thus thwarted his manipulations. Another makeup room battle exploded when Jackie and another woman were replaced by a new executive. By this time Cokie was getting sicker and weaker but again, she went to the mat for her friend, peppering her bosses with outraged emails. "She was not letting it go because she felt they were attacking two fifty-year-old women and she was not going to have it," recalls Jackie.

The exchanges got so heated that Jackie feared Cokie might be fired. "And she's like, they're not going to fire me, and if they do, they'll have another battle on their hands."

The women of ABC understood Cokie's value as their champion and defender and cheered her on. Linda Douglass says, "I don't know any other woman who the men were as afraid of as Cokie, and it was satisfying. It was amusing but mostly satisfying." Cokie also told women that they had to stand up for themselves, says Douglass: "She would say, 'Toughen up, remember who you are, you're an equal, you've got these skills and these powers. Don't take any shit from anybody.'" Barbara Fedida, then a producer at ABC, put Cokie's message to other women this way: "She showed you could be a badass without being a bitch."

While Cokie had some big public battles with her bosses and berated "the old guys above her" on personnel matters, much of what she did for other women consisted of small private acts of kindness and generosity. During one convention, recalls Jackie Walker, Cokie was assigned a suite in a fancy downtown hotel, but ABC's support staff and younger producers, including a woman named Shushannah Walshe, were given rooms far from the city center. "We had quick turnarounds and we weren't getting a lot of sleep," Walker recalls. "When she found out about Shush having these crazy work times she said, 'Come over and stay in my suite with me.' And then she told me, 'There's a couch, but if I'm not there, crawl into my bed, here's the room key, get breakfast, do whatever you need to do, but you're not going back to your hotel during the day.' There were several mornings when Cokie and I were both sleeping in her bed and it saved me an hour and a half, two hours travel time."

While Cokie was telling her sisters in the workforce to "toughen up" and "don't take any shit from anybody," she was sending them another powerful message as well: don't forget you're a woman, don't give up our traditional roles, you can have both a successful career and a successful family. At the time, it was an extraordinarily useful—and unusual—message. Many of the women who had succeeded in network TV were known, somewhat disparagingly, as "news nuns," women who felt they had to sacrifice their personal happiness to advance professionally. With a long marriage, two children, and eventually six grandchildren, Cokie was living proof of what she kept telling young women: I did it and you can too. Barbara Fedida was married, but had no children, when Cokie first came to ABC and encouraged her to start a family (she now has three children): "Cokie was one of the people who would say things like, you'll see, being a mom will make you a better producer or being a mom will make you better at your job for all these reasons that you can't understand until you get there. So she was actually one of the people who made me feel better about starting a family because I definitely was on the fence and I think that my husband was more eager to do that than I was. She had a really nice way of putting it in context." Lauren Burke, who served as Cokie's assistant, said so many people sought her advice "it was almost like she had a shingle outside her door," advertising therapy sessions.

The "fallopian jungle" from NPR days had been transplanted to Cokie's office at ABC. Men were occasionally welcome in that special space, but mainly they listened from outside the door and wondered what those women were talking about inside. Says David Glodt, who produced *This Week* for several years, "There was always a giggle coming from her office."

When Lauren Burke was Cokie's assistant, she was still attending American University and failing a math class she needed to graduate. "Cokie was almost like a third parent," recalls Burke. "I'm thinking to myself—because, when you're in your twenties, you think dumb things like this—why am I spending two thousand on a class I'm failing that I don't even need to have a job at ABC? And Cokie kept on me. She was worse than my parents. She kept on me to pass that class and kept saying, you know, you've got to get your degree. Not getting your degree, that wasn't even allowed to be a conversation." Cokie finally took matters into her own hands, as Lauren recalls: "She physically goes to the school to talk to one of my professors to say, OK, what does she have to do to pass this class? Is there any extra credit thing she should be doing? I was of course mesmerized by this because I didn't even know you could have that conversation." Burke eventually did get her degree and says now: "Part of the magic of Cokie is someone sitting there telling you that you can do something that you don't think you can do. She was like a magnet for people who needed not only advice but encouragement in a very tough competitive company."

Many of the young women Cokie worked with on *This Week*

were single, and on Sunday mornings "she genuinely loved hearing all of our funny stories about our Saturday-night dates. She was really like one of the girls," says Ilana Marcus Drimmer. But when a relationship turned serious, so did Cokie, and the women all wanted her stamp of approval "because we all knew Cokie was able to see through people. And it was like, if Cokie didn't approve, this thing wasn't going to fly." Ilana recalls the scene after she brought a special boyfriend to meet Cokie: "Everybody wanted to know what she thought of him, especially me, I wanted her to like him. And she did. So I married him." As these women found partners and contemplated marriage, Cokie always referred to her own relationship in offering advice. "She would talk about you," Ilana told me, and "she would always say, make sure you marry a man you're absolutely crazy about. That's the expression she would use, 'crazy about.' And she would tell us, make sure that he makes you laugh, because life is hard, it throws you a lot of things you don't know, so make sure you're crazy about him. Can you just picture her saying that?"

Cokie's devotion to babies was legendary, and that included showing up at every baby shower, no matter what else was going on. Karen Travers, who started as a college intern at ABC and eventually became a White House correspondent, says:

"Cokie was so busy, and yet she popped up to the seventh-floor conference room with a gift for whoever was about to go on maternity leave. She was part of the fabric of the bureau in a way that I think many people would be surprised to learn. She would bring great books for all the baby showers, that she thought the kids absolutely needed to have on their library shelf. And that was so important for all the young women to see, that you didn't just become super famous and super prominent and you're on another level than everybody else. She was still taking care of all of us."

Sara Just was a producer at *Nightline* when she first worked with Cokie, who liked to do needlework during meetings and embroidered special pieces for each of our grandchildren. Sara describes a familiar scene: "So she would bring her stitch work to a meeting and be sitting there, around a conference table stitching away, and it just cracked me up. She was doing this very female thing in front of all the guys. She and I would often talk about cooking, she was a great cook, and we would swap recipe ideas and sometimes we'd be alone in the conference room doing that. She'd be stitching and we'd be talking about cooking and then the men would walk in and I would say shush, like we shouldn't be talking about this here. And she once told me, 'We're women. We shouldn't be uncomfortable talking about the things we enjoy just because there are men in the room.' Then she winked and said something like, you know, it makes them uncomfortable and that's okay. It was such a great reminder and I really held that with me. Women in the workplace don't have to be more like men to fit in. They should be who they are, and she was just a great role model of that."

In all these ways, Cokie provided a "road map" for young women, says Ilana Drimmer, a role model for what a full, rich life looks like: independence and partnership, children and career, caring for yourself and caring for others. Her message was, "This is what strong important intelligent successful women do. You'd want to be in that club, because that was the club she was in." Tom Bettag said it even more simply: "People wanted to be like Cokie."

In 1996, David Brinkley retired from *This Week* and Cokie and Sam took over as coanchors. The pairing, says Bob Murphy, "was not going to work from the beginning. As Sam has proven time and time again, he is not an anchor, and he's certainly not an anchor when he's paired with someone else. His personality is just not conducive to an easy, comfortable dynamic relationship, especially on air." By 2002, Murphy says, Cokie "had been telling people for a long time that this wasn't working" and she decided to leave the show. She'd been working every Sunday for many years, and she wanted her weekends back. At the time I was a regular panelist on CNN's Sunday show, and she made me promise to quit at the same time she did, so we'd both be free of weekend obligations. CNN changed formats and actually ended my role a few months before her tenure was up, and she said, with typical insight into a male ego, "I'm sorry you got fired but I'm actually relieved because I never thought you'd keep your end of the bargain." Many people thought she left the show because of her breast cancer, but the timing was totally coincidental. She was editing the press release announcing her departure the same day she received her diagnosis. Over the next seventeen years she continued to contribute to many ABC shows, including *This Week* and live event coverage and as Bob Murphy notes her career "actually flourished" after she was no longer tied down by the Sunday show. In fact she still had two more outstanding careers ahead of her. Her first bestseller, *We Are Our Mothers' Daughters*, had been published in 1998, and she went on to write five more books, two we did together about our interfaith marriage and three that highlighted the contributions women had made to American history. She also shifted her contractual status at ABC, becoming a contributor instead of a full-time employee, and that change freed her up to become much more of a public advocate for causes she cared about, especially those benefitting women and children.

One event highlights the stature Cokie achieved as a journalist. In 2013, former president George W. Bush and his wife, Laura, were hosting a summit meeting in Tanzania featuring First Ladies from across Africa. Coincidentally, President Obama and his wife, Michelle, were going to be in Africa at the same time, and it was decided that the two American women would appear together during the meeting. But in what format? "We all agreed, yep, a conversation would be great, that would be fun, it would make a lot of sense," recalled Kristin King, then running advance for Mrs. Bush. "And so, then you get into, well, who should moderate this conversation?" Team Bush suggested a few names to Team Obama, and one stood out. "Cokie was the one person everybody could agree on," recalled Anita McBride, Mrs. Bush's longtime chief of staff. "It was sort of one of those aha, slam dunk moments. Mrs. Obama's team was absolutely comfortable with her from the get-go. And there was no discussion about anybody else after that. Cokie was the glue that helped bring this whole thing together."

It all happened so quickly that Cokie's name wasn't even included in the official program. As she recalled: "I'm at the beach, and I got a call from the Bush people saying, can you be in Tanzania next week? And I said, no. And then I told my husband and he said, why can't you be in Tanzania next week? Okay, I'll go to Tanzania. And I called ABC and said, can you find a way to send me to Tanzania? And they said, oh sure. And so off to Tanzania I went and interviewed the two of them and it was terrific." So terrific that she moderated two more conversations between the two First Ladies over the next few years. In one of my favorite photos, which is still on my desk, Cokie's onstage with Laura and Michelle, and the three of them are shaking with laughter. Says McBride: "There's kind of an unspoken understanding amongst people like Cokie and her family, the Bushes and their family, the Obamas, whoever makes that leap to be in elective office. Unless you've walked in those shoes, you really can't truly understand what it's like and know the responsibilities and challenges that come with it. The way that Cokie was able to draw all of those things out of these two well-known women, Michelle Obama and Laura Bush, and make them appear so human to everybody that was there—it was remarkable and just perfectly done."

Cokie never lost her love for live broadcasting, even when new anchors and executives at ABC did not always seem to understand her value. "They always wanted the new shiny thing that somebody else had," says Leslee Sherrill, then an ABC executive.

"I think the hard part was that Cokie had to keep proving herself over and over again." That's true, and Cokie did feel bruised at times by the ABC brass, but she was absolutely determined to stay active, even as her cancer returned in the summer of 2016. She told few people and often remarked, "It's hard enough being a 75-year-old woman on television, if you're a sick 75-year-old they'll never put you on." By the summer of 2019, she was noticeably thinner and weaker, but when *This Week* asked her to appear in August she eagerly accepted. She sent her friend Lynn Sherr an email with a brief reference to her illness: "All really tedious but bearable. Doing the show tomorrow. Thank heaven it's there." She was in denial; she didn't think the audience would notice her physical decline, but they did, and ABC had to issue a statement saying she had been sick but was recovering. Unfortunately, that was not true. She never appeared on television again. ABC was hosting a Democratic debate in Houston on September 12, and she was desperate to go. She even had Jackie Walker buy her new clothes, to accommodate her weight loss, but she was too sick to make the trip to Texas. She died five days later.

CHAPTER FIVE

Friend

"She held everybody up."

Cokie's friendships were deeply important to her. She understood that real relationships require time and tending, attention and affection. She did something to help a friend every single day of her life, and on many days, she did many things: wrote a note, made a call, sent a check, delivered a gift, offered a hug, held a hand, shared a meal, comforted a child, gave a talk, answered an appeal. Her door, and her heart, were always open. Her patience seemed inexhaustible and her advice invaluable. She showed up when her friends birthed their babies and buried their parents. She counseled them on choosing partners and raising families, confronting bosses and switching careers. As she got older, she extended her reach to her friends' children, remembering their names and birthdays, their schools and jobs. One of her most consistent commitments was visiting patients in the hospital. I used to joke that Cokie felt qualified to practice several medical specialties—oncology, obstetrics, even orthopedics— but in fact countless friends (and friends of friends) benefitted from her knowledge and leaned on her for support. She was particularly helpful to new mothers—"You know, babies don't break," she would tell them. And she regularly reached out to women newly diagnosed with cancer. She knew that when people receive that dread news, they are often so stunned and stressed that they are not thinking clearly, and need an advocate at their side to ask questions, listen to the answers, and represent their interests. Linda Winslow recounts what happened after her surgery for ovarian cancer: "The surgeon told me afterwards, he came out and Cokie was asking him questions. She was ferocious in her protection of me, because I didn't have any family at the time down here to do that. She was badgering this surgeon and he said, I felt like I was on *Meet the Press* because I kept ducking all these questions, thinking, my God, what am I in for here? I wanted to correct him and say wrong network, but I thought, oh, what the hell." Carol Klinger, a producer at NPR who switched doctors and treatment after consulting Cokie, says simply, "I realized she probably saved my life."

That's why so many women thought they had a special relationship with Cokie. That's why Bob Murphy sat at her funeral

The Boggs family at the Capitol, with Cokie holding her father's hand. The family business was politics, and this building shaped her entire life. *(Roberts family photo)*

Cokie as a teenager with her father, Hale, who was the majority leader of the House when he died in a plane crash while campaigning for a fellow lawmaker in 1972. *(Margery Lewis)*

Working on the yearbook at Stone Ridge, the Catholic school run by Sacred Heart nuns "who take girls seriously—a radical notion in the 1950s," as Cokie put it. She is in the center, and on her left is her lifelong friend Cinda Pratt Perlman. *(Roberts family photo)*

This portrait of Cokie was taken around the time we met in 1962, when she was eighteen and I was nineteen. The initials on her dress stand for her given name, Corinne Claiborne Boggs. (*Roberts family photo*)

Cokie at her first job, producing the high school quiz show *It's Academic*. (*Roberts family photo*)

At twenty-one, Cokie was hosting her own show, *Meeting of the Minds*, on the local NBC affiliate in Washington. Her guest that week was the secretary of education, Francis Keppel. (*Ernie Newhouse*)

President and Mrs. Johnson attended our wedding in the garden of Cokie's girlhood home in September 1966. We bought it from her mother in 1977 and lived there together for forty-two years.

When we moved to California in 1974, Cokie produced a children's show, *Serendipity*, for the local NBC station. (*Roberts family photo*)

During our California years, we started writing magazine articles together, and Cokie called the experience a "one-man journalism school." *(Geoffrey P. Fulton)*

At our mountaintop home in California, I toss Becca in the air while Cokie, Lee, and Lindy watch. *(Roberts family photo)*

Cokie with the kids on the edge of our patio in California overlooking the Pacific Ocean. A lovely view, but the isolation caused her to feel pretty lonely at times. *(Roberts family photo)*

When we moved to Greece, Cokie traveled with me on many assignments, including this visit to the ruins of an ancient settlement in Turkey. *(Roberts family photo)*

Cokie went to work for NPR and covered election night 1984 with Linda Wertheimer. *(Stan Barouh/ NPR)*

We both started
covering Congress—
she for NPR, me
for the *New York
Times*—and we
were often asked
to speak together.
(Roberts family photo)

Our basset hound,
Abner, became a
folk hero after he
interrupted Cokie's
broadcast on NPR one
Monday morning.
Our cat, Tabasco,
was less interested.
(Roberts family photo)

The Boggs Women: Cokie with her mother, Lindy, and sister, Barbara, who lost an eye to cancer and died at age fifty-one. *(Roberts family photo)*

A deeply devout Catholic, Cokie met Pope John Paul II a number of times during her mother's tenure as ambassador to the Vatican in the late '90s. *(© Foto Felici)*

The Dalai Lama gives Cokie a blessing after she interviewed him at Southern Methodist University in Dallas. *(Laura Buckman/AFP/ Getty Images)*

The Washington Post

Magazine

HER BRILLIANT CAREERS

Cokie Roberts ✤ *By Paul Hendrickson*

After Cokie moved her base from NPR to ABC, a number of magazines wrote cover stories about her, including this one from the *Washington Post*. This is my favorite photograph—those eyes look right through you—and it has hung on my office wall for years.
(© Frank Ockenfels III/ CPi syndication)

Cokie and I always enjoyed writing together, and this photo appeared with a cover story on interfaith marriage we did for *USA Weekend* on Easter Sunday 1997. That led to a book we coauthored, *From This Day Forward*, a few years later.
(© Claudio Vazquez, 1997)

One of Cokie's specialties was covering the Catholic Church, and she reported from the Vatican many times for ABC. *(Craig Sjodin/© ABC/ Getty Images)*

Another of her specialties was analyzing big events, like election nights. Here she instructs Sam Donaldson and Peter Jennings, the network's prime anchor. *(ABC Photo Archives/ © ABC/Getty Images)*

During her early days at ABC, Cokie and her Wellesley friend Lynn Sherr were often the only two women to appear on election night coverage. *(Courtesy of Lynn Sherr)*

After appearing on ABC's Sunday show for many years as a commentator, Cokie started hosting the show with Sam Donaldson in 1996. *(Terry Ashe/ © ABC/Getty Images)*

When First Ladies Michelle Obama and Laura Bush appeared together in Tanzania in 2013, the only moderator both sides could agree on was Cokie. She went on to preside over three such conversations. *(Grant Miller/ George W. Bush Presidential Center)*

Cokie's sharp wit made her a popular guest on many television talk shows, including *The View*. She was also a character in a *Saturday Night Live* sketch and the answer to many crossword puzzle clues. *(Lou Rocco/ © ABC/Getty Images)*

Growing up in the "family business" of politics, Cokie met—and often interviewed—all twelve presidents since John F. Kennedy. Here she chats with Bill Clinton at a Washington dinner. *(AP Photo/ Doug Mills)*

To Cokie — *with thanks for great dinner conversation and admiration for being smart enough to leave before the speeches started!* Bill Clinton
3-93

Nancy Pelosi, the first woman Speaker, is an old family friend who asked to speak at Cokie's funeral. *(AP Photo/Pablo Martinez Monsivais)*

Cokie and her mother in the Lindy Claiborne Boggs Congressional Women's Reading Room, the only room in the Capitol named for a woman. *(Ted Jackson/ The Times-Picayune/The New Orleans Advocate)*

We were very fortunate to have grandchildren while we were still young. Cokie throws out the first pitch at an Oakland As game with the help of Becca's twins, Jack and Cal Hartman. As her pink shirt indicates, she was raising awareness about breast cancer, a cause she championed long before her own diagnosis.
(Jed Jacobsohn/Getty Images Sport)

Cokie took total delight in our six grandchildren. Here she shares a laugh with our oldest, Regan, who was clever enough to get herself born on my fifty-eighth birthday. *(Roberts family photo)*

All six grandchildren and their parents surround Cokie and me at her mother's ninetieth birthday party in 2006. *(Roberts family photo)*

Cokie was a regular visitor to maternity wards and always told young moms "babies don't break." She holds the newborn of A. B. Stoddard, then a young producer at ABC. *(Courtesy of A. B. Stoddard)*

Cokie always loved spending time with our grandchildren at our beach house in South Carolina. She would rise early with our youngest, Cecilia, pictured here, and watch the "big red ball" rise out of the ocean. *(Roberts family photo)*

Her five bestselling books made Cokie an expert on women's history. She speaks in the Capitol rotunda at an event celebrating women's suffrage with our daughter, Rebecca, also an accomplished teller of women's stories. *(Kristie Baxter, House Creative Services)*

As an ardent advocate for the welfare of women and children, Cokie visited countries like Bangladesh, representing Save the Children, the worldwide relief organization. *(Shafiqul Alam Kiron/Save the Children)*

We celebrated our fiftieth wedding anniversary in 2016 on the exact same spot in the garden of our home where we'd been married. *(Roberts family photo)*

The *New York Times* interviewed us for their Love column in December 2017 and illustrated the story with this photo, taken on our back porch. *(Jared Soares / New York Times / Redux)*

The entire family gathers for a sunset cruise in Jamaica to mark Cokie's seventy-fifth birthday on December 27, 2018. *(Roberts family photo)*

and wondered how one person could have "several thousand" best friends. I talked to more than fifty of them, and I heard the same answers, the same stories, over and over again. Also the same word. Love. As Marcia Burick, a friend from Wellesley, put it, "I don't think I've ever known anybody who had so much love for people. Real love. Just incredible." Nina Totenberg, her fellow Founding Mother at NPR, says, "Those of us who were lucky enough to have been her friend will probably never have a friend like that ever again. She never forgot us. She always remembered us, whether it was in her first book or in her daily life or in any speech that she gave, we were never forgotten. And I try to learn that lesson from her."

Barbara Boggs Sigmund

Cokie's older sister, Barbara, was her first friend. "All my life she had been there, lording it over me and loving me, pushing me around and protecting me," Cokie wrote in *We Are Our Mothers' Daughters*. "Those elusive early childhood memories that shimmer to the surface when summoned all involve her. Running to her when the dog next door jumped up and grabbed my two-year-old hair in its teeth. Barbara running to our mother complaining that if I insisted on putting on doll clothes, couldn't I be confined to the backyard. Going to school where she, four years older, shepherded me from room to room. Getting her out of class to pull my baby teeth. Huddling together against the brother between us in age, the common enemy." When Barbara died from cancer in 1990, at age fifty-one, Cokie was with her. After Barbara took her last breath in the middle of the night, Cokie got into the bed, holding her dead sister in her arms and singing to her until dawn broke and it was time to deal with the grim details of death.

While Cokie was deeply devoted to her sister, there was always an undercurrent of tension between them. "Barbara excelled at everything, always. But I don't ever remember being jealous of her," Cokie wrote. "I just desperately wanted to please her, and I often didn't. She had the ability to push all of my buttons, the way most women (including my daughter) complain their mothers do." The older sister was mainly a product of the 1950s, the younger of the 1960s. That helped make Cokie somewhat less rigid and more tolerant, and the difference showed itself in many ways, including their attitude toward religion. Barbara was briefly engaged to a Jewish man, Allard Lowenstein, but the relationship foundered in part because they could not reconcile their different faiths. Cokie's friend Cinda Perlman told me: "I think that affected Cokie in a fairly profound way because I think she felt her sister, who went on to have a good marriage and all of that . . . maybe had given up the love of her life. And Cokie did not want to give up the love of her life. And I think she figured there must be a way through this that Barbara did not figure out, and I'm going to figure it out."

Barbara eventually married Paul Sigmund, one of my political science professors from Harvard who had moved on to Princeton. While Cokie never joined the "family business" of politics, Barbara did with gusto, winning election as mayor of Princeton and serving for seven years until her death. Whatever tension existed between the sisters quickly dissipated when Barbara, who had lost an eye to cancer years before, was diagnosed with a recurrence. "During this illness, Cokie has been spectacular," Barbara told *People* magazine. "She leaves important assignments all over the country to be with me. She calls up and is her dear funny self." While Barbara was receiving chemotherapy treatments in a Philadelphia hospital, Cokie moved into her room, and Barbara wrote this poem:

She called herself
My "private duty sister."
And so she was.
Day and, most especially,
Terror-bearing night,
She will always appear
As a vision,
Her glorious almond-shaped eyes
Shut in a beautiful arc,
Guarding me even in her glancing sleep.

There was always a bantering quality to the sisters' relationship, and Cokie recalled the scene the day before Barbara died: "Barbara and I had a good laugh as I was combing her hair, which hadn't been colored in a while. 'I think we're seeing your natural hair color for the first time since you were fifteen,' I teased." But they also had a deeply serious conversation, a conversation that eventually caused Cokie more anguish than almost anything else in her life. She promised Barbara she would take care of her three sons, then all in their twenties. The oldest, Paul Jr., was a brilliant young lawyer who had always displayed a taste for risk-taking, and after he moved to San Francisco with his wife and two young daughters he became a drug addict. As his career and marriage crumbled, Cokie did everything possible to keep her promise, paying for endless and fruitless rounds of rehab and refusing to lose touch. "It upset and frustrated her so much that no matter what she did, it didn't work," says Barbara's youngest son, Stephen. "I told her, 'You're doing everything you can, you've done so much. No one else has committed to him and still believed in him in the way that you have. But it's got to be him who does it, right? It's got to be him who takes the responsibility. You can't fix it.'" But Cokie never quite believed that she couldn't "fix it" with Paul, and when he spiraled downward and finally died in jail, she was totally distraught, calling a relative and sobbing, "I've failed my sister." It wasn't true. "There is no one on earth who should have felt less guilt than Cokie around my brother," says Stephen. "She did everything possible she could have done." She kept her promise, but her sense of failure never fully faded.

Her grief over Barbara's death never fully faded either. Cokie remembers exploding with outrage over an article about post-menopausal women having babies, and picking up the phone to call her sister: "Ready to have a good giggle, I dialed her number before I remembered she wouldn't be there to share my astonishment. The shock of her absence made me feel very alone." In 1994, to mark thirty years after her college graduation, Cokie composed a brief reflection for her Wellesley classmates that invoked the impact of Barbara's death: "It never occurred to me that my sister wouldn't be in the next rocking chair on the nursing home porch. The image of that empty chair often serves now as a guide." And Cokie's empty chair now serves as a guide to many of her friends.

Cinda Pratt Perlman

Barbara and Cinda's older sister Claire were friends, and Cinda says, "I kept hearing about this really great little sister Barbara had, an awful lot better little sister than poor Claire had been stuck with, and I thought, well, lah-dee-dah, maybe she's great and all of that, but too bad you have me." One day Cinda and Claire were meeting a group of girls in the parking lot of a local church and Cokie was there too. "I think Claire said, 'Oh look, there's Cokie, now you can meet her' and this totally vivacious burst of energy person comes skipping over to me, grabs my arm, and says, 'Cinda, I've been waiting to meet you,' and I thought, oh my God, what is this? I was very shy, I found it very hard to meet new people, and here is this phenomenon who grabs my arm and pulls me in some direction and I just had no choice but to go with her. And that is how we met." Cokie was ten, and they remained friends for the next sixty-five years.

They wound up at the same Catholic girls' school, Stone Ridge, and a year or two later they were attending a school meeting together, sitting on folding chairs, and Cokie did something Cinda has never forgotten: "When it ended, people got up and went back to their classes or whatever was next. And I started to do that and Cokie said, where are you going? And I said, I'm going back, we have such and such a class. And she said, not before we put these chairs away. And I said, us? And she said, who do you think is going to do it? And I thought, okay, I get it. You're right. And so we just went to work and folded up all those chairs."

They did everything together, including singing, and "we had a crush on the same nun, Mother Whelan," Cinda recalls. "We used to corner her and stand there singing 'You Are My Sunshine' in two-part harmony." They had a pact to attend the same college, and during their freshman year at Wellesley, Cokie tried out for a singing group, the Widows, and was immediately accepted. Cinda, however, was rejected, and dejected, and wanted to quit. But Cokie insisted she try out again. "I did, and I got in, and I wouldn't have done it if she hadn't said, just don't give up so easily," Cinda recalled. When I asked why they had remained such good friends for so long, she replied: "Cokie would really listen to you. She would make you feel like at that moment, you're the most important thing in her life, and she's there for you." Cokie was there for her some years later when Cinda, the sister of a nun, rather suddenly decided to marry the son of a rabbi. The ceremony came together quickly, and it was Cokie who insisted they make a Jewish chuppah for the couple to be married under. The two Catholic girls who had met in that church parking lot years before, and had a crush on the same nun, had come a long way.

Courtney Manard Kane and Jo Pepper Morrison Tuepker

When a new assistant started working for Cokie, she was usually presented with a three-page, handwritten family tree. Memorize this, she was told, and if anybody on this list ever calls me, put them right through. That diagram reflects the importance Cokie placed on her family connections. A boss or big shot may get placed on hold but never a relative, and two of the most important names on the tree were female cousins close to Cokie in age: her city cousin, Courtney Manard, who lived in New Orleans, and her country cousin, Jo Pepper Morrison, who lived along the Gulf Coast of Mississippi. Both women tell a similar story. After Cokie's sister, Barbara, died she said to each of them, now you have to be my sister.

"There was never a time when I didn't know Cokie, that we were not part of each other's lives," says Courtney. When the girls were four, Courtney was enrolled in a local preschool run by Miss Edith Aiken, leaving Cokie without her playmate. Hale and Lindy were away, and Cokie was living with relatives, so one day she simply walked the several blocks to Miss Aiken's and enrolled herself in classes. When Lindy returned a few weeks later she was horrified: the school was far too expensive for the family budget, but her mother gamely volunteered to pay Cokie's fees. Recalls Courtney: "Miss Aiken said, 'Oh no, she enrolled herself and we have come to an understanding, so she's welcome to stay.'"

"I'm sure it will not surprise you to find that Cokie knew how to take advantage of the rules," Courtney goes on. "One of those summer days when she was living with us, my mother served bacon and eggs for breakfast. Cokie really liked the bacon, and in those days meat was supposed to be off the Catholic menu on Friday. And I remember distinctly her saying, one lovely Friday, 'Please pass the bacon. I'm six. I haven't reached the age of reason yet.' Doesn't that sound exactly like her? She always knew her own mind." (Under Church doctrine, children who had not reached the "age of reason" did not have to obey adult rules.)

The cousins agreed on politics and spent many hours helping Hale's campaign efforts. "I don't know any other girls our age that hung out at political headquarters, but that's what we did, we tried to make ourselves useful," says Courtney. But religion was another matter. Since she was Episcopalian and Cokie was Catholic, "There were great religious arguments about if you weren't part of my religion, then you're surely condemned to go to hell. But Cokie could never bring herself to admit to us that she thought any such thing. She was sure there was an exception for particularly nice Episcopalians who were related to her."

"Besides being a cousin, she became a friend, she was just always there," says Jo Pepper. "She was kind of bossy. But she never really thought of herself as bossy." One summer, when they about ten, the cousins spent part of the summer with relatives at a plantation in northern Louisiana. They found a copy of the novel *Gone with the Wind* and Cokie announced that she would read it to Jo Pepper. But then she started asking her cousin questions, to see if she understood the plotline. "It would be like, let's check and make sure you're comprehending this," Jo Pepper recalls. "It's just the way she worked. She couldn't help it. She didn't do it in any derogatory way or anything like that. She just really felt she was being helpful. She was just being Cokie." Jo Pepper finally told her to stop the quizzes: "I felt like I was taking a test and I didn't particularly like tests, so let's cut out the test and get on with the reading." Jo Pepper became a therapist and says, "Looking back on it, we were really getting ready for our careers." In Cokie's profession, "you speak and people listen. In my career, people speak and I listen." Many years later, Cokie traveled to the Gulf Coast for the wedding of Jo Pepper's daughter Catherine. Hours before the ceremony, things seemed a bit disorganized, so Cokie, the "bossy" cousin, took over, telling the wedding party where to walk and how to act. The bride's maid of honor was a bit put out with this interloper, thinking Cokie was usurping her role. As Jo Pepper recalls, "So she turns to Catherine and says, 'Who is that woman?'" Many others asked that question over the years. And they all found out.

Marcia Burick Goldstein

Marcia was a delegate from Wellesley to the National Student Association and attended the group's annual conference at the University of Minnesota in the summer of 1960. There she met Cokie's sister, Barbara, a delegate from Manhattanville, a Catholic women's college just north of New York City, and relates their conversation: "Barbara said, my little sister's going to Wellesley and she's very shy. She's only 16, she's gone to these schools with nuns, so keep an eye out for her." That might be the only time in her entire life anyone called Cokie "shy." Back at school that fall, Marcia arranged for herself to be appointed Cokie's "big sister," a Wellesley tradition of informal mentoring for incoming freshmen. The older girls organized a picnic to meet the newcomers and Marcia recalls: "In came Cokie with 10 immediate best friends she'd already made and took over the picnic. They came and overwhelmed us. I just remember her walking into that picnic, so adorable, and then I said, I'm your big sister and I'm here to help you in any way possible. And she said, well, what can I do to help you?"

Cokie soon did do something for Marcia, who was active in Democratic politics. She invited her to a rally John F. Kennedy was holding in the Boston Garden on the night before election day. "She said to me, wear tennis shoes, and I said, oh no, you wear hose and heels to something like that, and she said, wear tennis shoes. When we got there it was so crowded we couldn't get through the turnstile, and she said, jump. And I said, I can't jump, and she said, that's why you're wearing tennis shoes! We jumped and we're with a million people, packed and pushed together, and we thought we're not going to get in. Then somebody she knew from the Kennedy campaign spotted her and said, come on down, and we sat in like the tenth row above the basketball court and it was amazing."

In November of 1989, Marcia's son Dan was attending Bates College in Maine and suffering severe emotional problems. A doctor prescribed a drug that can cause sudden suicidal impulses. Dan, who could not legally buy a drink in the state, walked into a gun store, purchased a weapon, returned to campus, and shot himself. "Cokie was there the next morning," recalls Marcia, who was living in Western Massachusetts. "Suddenly she walked in the door. I don't know who called her, I don't know how she got there but there she was." The funeral was at noon, and all morning "she just sat there as people came in" and greeted them. Many people are afraid of grief, and don't know what to say, but Cokie "held on to us, she never stopped holding on to us." As they drove to the funeral, Cokie sat with Marcia in the back of the car, "and she said to me, just pretend you're Nancy Reagan for the next few hours. Stiff upper lip. You know, be in control. She sat with me. It wasn't easy." At the graveside, "people have told me they remember that she held Kenny (Marcia's older son) on one side and me on the other. She held us both up. She held everybody up." The next spring, Cokie flew to Maine and gave a talk at Bates honoring Dan.

Martha Angle Walters

"If it weren't for Cokie, we probably never would have been married," says Martha, who met her husband, Bob, in the mid-'60s, when they were both young reporters on the old *Washington Star*. But after three years of dating and no proposal, Martha "just sort of lost patience" and "bailed out of the relationship." Several months later, Bob visited us in California, and Martha recounts what happened: "Cokie read him the riot act. She told him he was a damn fool to have let me go, and get himself back to DC and make it up forthwith. She really laid into him apparently and something stuck, it registered with him. He wrote me the one and only letter he ever wrote in his life. Basically, he said he was missing me and felt terrible. And would I please give him another chance. And I did. And here we are 50 years later. Cokie had an enormous belief in the importance of family, in the importance of marriage as an institution and the need for people to be together and to take care of each other and to look out for each other. She was a master matchmaker. She felt that people who she cared about and she thought were good for each other belonged together. And she was damn well going to make sure they got there."

Many years later, during a dinner at our house, Martha told us that she'd just been diagnosed with breast cancer. Cokie insisted on tearing up her schedule and taking her friend to an appointment with an oncologist. "I was just stunned, because I knew how swamped she was with work stuff," Martha recalled. "I had a list of questions that I had written out in advance but I hadn't been through this before. She let me run through my questions. And then she asked a few more and we walked out of the office together and we looked at each other and we both said at the exact same moment, I like him. And then we burst out laughing. It was such a huge relief because I think if she had said, I don't think so, I would have gone off and searched for somebody else. So I just felt at that moment that it was all going to be alright."

I tried to learn from Cokie how to nurture and nourish friend-ships, but connections between women have an intensity, and an intimacy, that male relationships seldom achieve. Says Martha: "There's a level of communication that's more than verbal, and the other person just gets it instantly because you've been there. You've done that. You've seen it. You've experienced it. And Cokie was just immensely empathetic. She was never invasive. She was just there for you."

Linda Cozby Wertheimer

When Cokie came to NPR in 1977, our children were seven and nine, and Linda had this reaction: "I was interested that she had kids because I had pretty much decided that this was not going to happen for me, that I couldn't afford to do it, I couldn't walk out and have a baby and expect to walk back in." Cokie offered a dif-ferent model: "I guess I'd been looking all the time at the things that I would not be able to do if I had kids, but she never looked at it that way, and that was revelatory for me." Linda was inspired to try to get pregnant, and when it didn't happen "I really mourned it, and I still feel very sorry that I don't have children." The ex-perience turned Linda into the kind of evangelist for parenthood that Cokie had always been: "I have always told young women who say, I just can't, I can't have a baby this year because I've just started this, and I say bullshit. Have a baby. There are laws against firing you because you're having a baby. You can do it. Go talk to Cokie.

"The other thing that Cokie did was share her mother with

me, which was a big deal, because I was a great distance from my mother and then my mother died," says Linda. Cokie's mother, Lindy, had moved back to Washington and met Linda many times at family events. When Linda faced serious surgery, and a possible cancer diagnosis, Cokie sent her mother to keep watch at Linda's bedside. "I woke up and there was Lindy standing by my bed holding my hand and I said, what happened?" says Linda. "And she said, you do not have cancer. You are going to be all right." She kept slipping in and out of consciousness over the next few hours, and Lindy stayed with her, the motherly presence Linda lacked in her own life. "Cokie was very lucky to have her for as long as she did," Linda told me. "And I think she felt very strongly that she was lucky in that way and she knew that would help me. So she did it."

Michel McQueen Martin

"I like to think of Cokie as Glinda the Good Witch from *The Wizard of Oz* who would pretend to be setting you on the right path, only to tell you that you knew the way all along," says Michel Martin, who today hosts the weekend version of *All Things Considered*. "Many times over the years when I was attacked for my reporting, a note would show up in my inbox out of the blue saying something like, 'You were absolutely right to ask that question. You handled yourself perfectly.' When Cokie and I were on the air together, in the greenroom or on the way to the studio, she would gently drop knowledge about everything from why she always walked to the studio instead of taking the elevator to navigating a two-career marriage to how to frame a sensitive question." Cokie was especially forceful in encouraging Michel to stand up to mendacious male bosses: "In essence, she would be saying, 'They aren't all powerful. They are not 10 foot tall. Don't let them get to you.' When I came here to NPR, the emails out of the blue continued: 'Your show was so good. The mix was great. The interview with so-and-so was spot on. Thanks for making us all look good.' When the first show I hosted at NPR was canceled, she showed up in the office, although she had no reason to, just to take me to lunch in the cafeteria as a statement of solidarity."

Lesley Stahl

Lesley, like Linda Wertheimer, believed she had to choose between personal satisfaction and professional success. But her first meeting with Cokie changed her mind and her life: "She persuaded me to have a child by proving that you could be an attentive mother as she was and have a big career. And then she helped me raise my daughter." In the mid-'70s, Lesley was a reporter for CBS and a close friend of one of Cokie's bridesmaids, Eden Lipson. She and her boyfriend Aaron Latham were planning a trip to Greece while we were stationed there, and Eden urged Lesley to look us up. She continues the tale: "I had not wanted a child. I thought I wouldn't have been a good mother. And my mother always told me not to have children by the way, because she said, quote, they'll ruin your life. Close quote. Thanks, Mom. But there was Cokie with these two gorgeous children and it began to change my thinking about the possibility of having a career and a family. It was powerful, and I got pregnant right after."

A year or two later we moved back to Washington, Lesley's daughter, Taylor, was a toddler, and the two women formed an enduring friendship. The new mother describes Cokie's role: "I always say that Cokie helped me raise Taylor. I would turn to her, I relied on her a lot. And of course, she was the one who gave Taylor a religious education. Here was a kid who was half Jewish and half Christian and Cokie took that over. I actually gave it to her. Here, I said, you educate Taylor, that's your job. And she did." Lesley and her family became regulars at our Chanukah parties and Passover Seders, where most of the guests were like us, interfaith couples. At the Seders, Taylor was a particularly enthusiastic participant in a song called "Rise and Shine," which involves a lot of raucous hand clapping. For years, long after Lesley had moved to New York to become a correspondent for the CBS show *60 Minutes*, Cokie would still insist on singing what she always called "Taylor's song."

While she was still in Washington, Lesley recruited Cokie to join other female reporters in a ladies' lunch group: "There were so few women covering politics that all of us fit around one small table. A lot of us were in newsrooms that were just overwhelmingly male, so a group of us decided that we desperately needed the company of women because we were living on strange planets at work, the conversations in our offices were all about sports and sports. There were certain ground rules. We wouldn't talk shop because we were all reporters, we wouldn't talk about the things we were covering. We would talk about our daily lives. We'd talk about our marriages, we would talk about shopping, we would talk about getting through the day. We would talk about the men at our offices, our problems. And we began, all of us, to crave these once-a-week lunches, they became almost sacred to us. I think we all came to see that more women sitting around in a circle and talking, talking, talking was an essential necessity." I asked Lesley about another ground rule: their adamant refusal to talk to other reporters about their group. "Well, we wanted to have our privacy," she replied. "And the whole point of it was that we could come and talk about anything we wanted. There was a dome of silence and we would protect each other and we laughed a lot. But Cokie was the one with wisdom, the one we all went to for advice. I'm actually older than she was, but I was the one who was looking up to her, as I think most of her women friends did. She had a moral authority that may have come out of her deep faith, but she was a force, not just because of the intelligence. She was the person you wanted to be like. She was a kind of moral glue and I mean moral in the best way."

Amy Entelis

Amy tells a story that I heard countless times from Cokie's friends, not just the women: "The first thing Cokie would ever say to me or to anybody else when she saw them is: How are your kids? Every single time. So that was a signal, an entree into a conversation about how they were doing, what the struggles were with them. Were they healthy? Where did they go to school? What time are you getting home? The overarching message of that conversation was your kids are as important, or more important than anything you're doing here and don't ever forget it. Don't regret the time you spend with them. Don't, don't, don't do things you don't have to do because you never get the time back. Cokie knew that I had two boys. She knew that they were named Luke and Dylan. She knew how old they were, she knew when they were starting school. She knew if they were going to summer camp. I don't know how she did that for so many people, honestly, like she had it all in her head and she was always able to reference something you told her two months before and she'd bring it up two months later and she'd ask you how it went or how was the first day of school or something like that. Cokie was the person who always taught me to put my kids first. And I know she did that with so many people."

Leslee Sherrill

Leslee was an ABC executive who, after many frustrating attempts to conceive a child, found herself pregnant with triplets. Her memory: "When I was expecting triplets, Cokie was the first person I called and said, what am I going to do? And she's like, you're going to be fine. Nothing was going to be wrong, it was going to go fine and they'll be fine. She just made me instantly feel a million times better about producing three children at once as only she could." When I asked why she had called Cokie first, Leslee responded: "Because she was a mom. There were a lot of news nuns around there, you know. And she knew I was trying to have a baby, she knew it was my second marriage, she knew this was going to be my last turn at bat, because we had shared all that. She just gave me the confidence that I could handle it, that I hadn't bitten off more than I could chew. She just assured me that it was a blessing and, oh my God, this is fantastic. And I just had a sense of calm, like it's going to be okay. And then the funny thing is, I think because I felt so good about it, I had the easiest pregnancy in the world. I felt great all the time. I gave birth to the three of them. I was like, wow, I'd do that again. That was not bad. And then my doctor sent me to every woman who turned out to be pregnant with triplets. And so I became the go-to to calm down all these nervous moms, but I really got my footing from those initial conversations with Cokie."

With Cokie's help, Leslee got a job at the University of Southern California, and when she was first asked to appear on a public panel discussion, she called her old friend for advice: "She told me exactly how to deal with male panelists because I was really nervous. I was the only woman on this panel. She told me exactly what to wear, everything." I asked Leslee what Cokie told her, and she replied: "Don't let them interrupt you. Be really polite. Don't wear man clothes. Wear a skirt. Be very clear that you are a female presence, that you have a perspective and you're not trying to blend in. You don't want to look like everybody else. Wear something comfortable and be assertive, get yourself in there, don't let them mow over you. So I just had a lot more confidence. And you know, it seems dumb, but what you wear and are comfortable in really does matter, because once you're confident about that you don't even think about it. So that was really, really helpful, I felt really good and I did many more panels after that. Cokie was always there when you needed her and you never ever felt like she was too busy. And then of course you'd see her 10 minutes later on the air knowing every single thing about everything happening on the Hill, and you're thinking, but she just spent 45 minutes with me on the phone. How is that possible?'"

Linda Douglass

Like Lesley Stahl, Linda credits Cokie with helping her raise her only child, her daughter, Katie: "I was always beside myself about my one daughter and Cokie would just laugh about it. I mean, she would just say, oh, come on, you're going to wind up planting a computer chip in your daughter, so you could see where she is all the time. Relax, it's fine. She's a great kid. And I just said, how do you know this? You don't know Katie. I'm about to quit my job. She's driving me nuts. I was convinced she was going to go to the dark side and marry some guy on a motorcycle and go off and I'll never see her again. But Cokie always believed in Katie, who turned out to be really good in science in her junior year of high school and Cokie said, see? I told you she was really smart. She's probably going to be a doctor. And Cokie got this book on Marie Curie, and the struggles she went through to be recognized as a groundbreaking scientist, which she gave me to give to Katie, and it's one of Katie's favorite books. She probably was going to turn out fine anyway, like Cokie said, but it didn't seem that way to me. Cokie was always so proud of Katie, she was a daughter and Cokie believed in the goodness of daughters and the importance of daughters." Katie did become a doctor, and holds a high position at a Washington-area hospital. Says Linda: "Cokie saw the real Katie. She saw my only daughter so much more clearly than I did."

Sonya McNair

Sonya was twenty-one, working at ABC as a receptionist while finishing college, when her cousin was murdered, leaving behind an infant named Larry. At first the child lived with his grandmother during the week and Sonya on weekends, but then the older woman died and Sonya found herself as Larry's full-time caretaker while still juggling work and school: "I went to Cokie, and told her what happened, and she immediately started giving me so much advice about what it's like to work in television and the kind of hours we were having to work and raise children and how to balance work-life issues. Just because she cared, not because of any other reason, just out of sheer love for me and care for my development. Whenever I would have a question about parenting or anything else, she would be my go-to person. I was feeling so guilty, I was concerned about the hours I worked, it meant that when Larry came home from school, I wasn't there immediately. And if there was a breaking news story, it would mean I got home late and that window of time, from when I got home until the time he had to go to bed was shrinking regularly and I was feeling so guilty, given the fact that he had lost his mom and then his grandmom. And the only mother he had was only spending this short window of time with him. My heart was so heavy and I remember Cokie saying, he's not going to remember the amount. He will remember the quality of time. So make the time you have with him count and make it quality time because that will matter most to him. And it just helped me tremendously because it was such a hard path, just trying to navigate and she helped me to see, do the best you can with what you have and don't focus on what you don't have. And it was just a wonderful moment of wisdom to help me to see things differently." When Larry was diagnosed with a learning disability, Sonya again consulted Cokie: "I went to her and I said, Cokie, I'm not sure. Do you think that they're saying these things because he's African American? Do you think that they would say it if it were their child? And I said, it's so hard to wonder if there was an inherent assumption that he couldn't learn or whatever. And then we walked through it. My mom and I did as well. But it was so nice to hear a second opinion just to make sure—sometimes you don't have anybody, some people don't have places to go, to someone who has such knowledge and wisdom who can help you, at any given time. But she always did. No matter what. She always did."

When Sonya got engaged, Cokie offered to have her wedding in our garden. And months before the day she called to say she'd planted flowers that would bloom in time for the ceremony, in colors that would match the dresses and decorations. "Who does that?" Sonya recalls. "Here she had this huge life and yet she cared about such small details." The wedding was scheduled for right after 9/11, so it never happened in our garden. But later in their relationship, Cokie did make it to the funeral for Sonya's brother, at one of Washington's oldest Black churches: "We were at the funeral, and Cokie just walked down the aisle. Out of nowhere she appeared and it was in the middle of the day. It meant so much to us that she would take the time to just show up and she hugged my mom so beautifully. Oh my goodness, it was almost like my two mothers hugging. My mom was so grateful for how Cokie had been so wonderful to me and it actually helped my whole family. It just warmed them. It just meant so much because there was so much hurting and that was a bright spot for them in the healing process."

Gloria Rivera

Gloria Rivera was a young producer at ABC when her father was visiting town and asked to meet Cokie. "I brought my father by, and she treated him like an old friend within seconds," says Gloria. "I sat next to my dad and they had this conversation about politics, and he was gobsmacked. I never saw my dad look like that in the presence of anyone really, he was so impressed, he'd say he was tickled. She really knew how to give these small acts of kindness that made me feel really safe in the news business." Rivera's father had been married four times, and later he said to his daughter: "I think maybe I should have been looking for a gal like Cokie." Gloria had stopped working to care for two small children, and she recalls what happened: "Cokie called and said, 'I'm coming over to see you and the babies,' and I was like 'Oh shit,' I mean I was delighted to see her, but I was feeling pretty low about stuff then. My husband vacuumed, we had the tiniest house and Cokie came over, and she had gifts for the kids and we sat on my couch and it was one of those, okay, tell me everything conversations. My own perspective as a new mother and a woman in news was that it was just all too much and she could totally relate. And I remember she looked at me and said, 'It's time to get back to work.' I felt like she was sending me a very clear signal, 'I'm telling you this because it'll be good for you.' And when I heard that, I realized I had really lost my sense of professional identity. I was sitting there with a baby on my hip and a toddler at my knee and spit-up on my shirt and dirty bottles in the sink. And it was like all of a sudden, 'Oh man, I want to go back to work.' And later we would have conversations about the fact that being working mothers made us better people. She saw me as both, right? Reporter and mother. That day on the couch, when I didn't have one shred of confidence, the question in my head was, who am I to think that I can do this? And Cokie was there with the answer, which was, who are you *not* to do this?"

Ilana Marcus Drimmer

Ilana Marcus Drimmer worked with Cokie at *This Week* and recalls the message she sent to young women at ABC: "Cokie never apologized, or felt bad about being a woman. She really believed in so many ways that being a woman made her superior in terms of working. The story that she told all the time, which I still talk about, is that men cannot multitask. They are hunters. They get out in the bush and they hunt for that lion. But women, she would say, women have to cook the dinner—she would do a whole thing with her arms, making a big pot that she would stir. Then she'd take her foot and give it a kick and say, then they have to kick away the lion. And they have to nurse the baby. And they do it all at the same time. That's why we're the best multitaskers. She gave a biological reason why being a working mother and a working woman was an asset, that our brains were wired to multitask. And I always think about that because, first of all it makes perfect sense. And second of all it gave the women who were younger than Cokie such a sense of power, that our brains were actually wired to be working women, and we wanted to emulate her. She always said, we hire the moms, they know how to get everything done, and it was true."

Cokie's words, and experience, sent a clear message to her young friends: know your power, appreciate your possibilities, being a woman should be an asset, not a drawback—a strength, not a weakness. And part of being a woman means caring for others. Ilana recalls that when she turned thirty, Cokie gave her a pearl necklace: "Who would imagine that somebody that famous and successful would remember a young person's birthday, but it wasn't even a question that she would remember it. It was who Cokie was, she had time and space for everyone." When Ilana went wedding dress shopping with her mother, Cokie assailed her with questions when she returned: "She wanted every detail. She wanted to know where we went and what would I choose and when I was trying on my dress, I kind of had Cokie in mind

because I knew she would be so excited about it. She really cared."
And when Ilana had her first child, she describes what happened
when Cokie showed up at the hospital after getting off the air:
"All she cared about was getting her hands on my baby, she loved
babies so much. So she said, 'Give me that baby.' And she looked
at me and said, 'I hope you don't mind if I do this,' and she lifted
her finger and gave him a quick baptism, just in case. He was a
Jewish boy but of course I didn't mind because you know, as she
said, you just want to cover all your bases."

Jane Aylor

Cokie had the gift of showing up at times, and in places, where
others felt uneasy. If hospital rooms were a specialty, so were funerals and wakes. She was comfortable dealing with death because she had suffered so much loss in her own life. Jane was
helping to run ABC's Washington bureau when her brother died
suddenly in 2004: "He was my younger brother. I adored him, he
died suddenly of a heart attack and I was devastated. So when I
came back to work, Cokie just appeared in my office one day and
sat down and said, how are you feeling? I know this is terrible.
I've lost a sibling. I do understand what you're going through.
And I just burst into tears. She got up and closed the door and
I just walked through the whole thing with her about how I got
the news—the disbelief, the immeasurable sadness, and Cokie
just let me talk. And I kept saying to her, Cokie, I know you're
so busy, you don't need to sit and listen to this. And she said, you
are the most important person to me and I'm not busy at all and

I want you to just keep talking. And she probably stayed for an hour, Steve. It meant the world to me."

That would not be the last time the two women bonded over the death of a loved one. Jane and her husband, Jim, were practicing Episcopalians, but her mother-in-law was a devout Catholic, and when she died, Jane described their dilemma: "We were trying to find a Catholic church that would do the funeral for her, but she was living in an assisted living facility. She didn't actually belong to a church up here as she did in Florida before she moved, so we could not find a church that would do the service for her. So I said to Jim, I've got to talk to Cokie because maybe she'll have a suggestion. So I called Cokie and she just sputtered. This is outrageous, this is just outrageous! I'm going to call the cardinal or whatever. And I said, no, Cokie, no, I don't want you to do that. I just want some guidance. What do you think? And she said, all right, sit tight. I'm going to make a call. I'll get back to you. So she called me back and she said, all right, I've called a dear friend of mine, Father Bill George, and he has agreed to do the service at your church with your minister. He will sort of co-officiate. And she said, here's his number. He's waiting for your call. So I called Father George and he said, no worries. I can do this. I actually know Bill Hague, your minister, I'll get in touch with Bill, I can be there, I can say some things, we'll make it work. And they did. It was just a beautiful service, and it was all due to Cokie." Jane met Father George again years later when they served on the same charitable board: "And I said, Father George, you probably don't remember me, but Cokie Roberts enlisted you to help with my mother-in-law's funeral a few years ago. And he said, you know what, Jane? I have to say, I probably don't remember because Cokie enlisted me so often to help with her friends. And he said, I was always happy to do it. There was nobody like Cokie and there will never be another Cokie."

Donna Brazile

Cokie met Donna, a longtime Democratic strategist, when they started appearing together on ABC's Sunday-morning roundtable. They bonded over their common ties to New Orleans, their love of the Saints, their devotion to Tabasco, and their cousins in Mississippi. "We always found time to drag on them because they were from Mississippi," Donna says. "And they somehow seemed to all be the same regardless of the fact that one was a set of Blacks and the other a set of whites." Donna never married, and had no children of her own, and it was Cokie who encouraged her to support her young relatives financially. "Over the last 30 odd years, I don't know the number of nieces and nephews I've put through Catholic schools in and around New Orleans because of Cokie," she says. "Whenever someone couldn't take care of a kid and I knew they had potential, I would call Cokie and say, here's this one. She's five years old, she's very smart, or he's seven years old, he's getting bullied in school. And she said, send him to the church. You want me to call the Archbishop? Get them in a school, Donna, how much is it? And I would tell Cokie, and she said, that's nothing compared to how much it is in DC. Put them in school, you'll feel better later. Now that was Cokie.

And when they graduated, I'd always show her the picture. And when she passed away and I went back and looked at all of our emails and all of our conversations, it was always personal. It was about family and friends and relatives. When Cokie died, when I was there, in that church, I was crying because I said, 'Cokie, I ain't got no more tuitions. I'm done.'"

After Hurricane Katrina devastated New Orleans, Cokie urged Donna to buy picture frames made from wood that had been salvaged from the storm: "I keep her picture on my mantelpiece. All the Louisiana people were trying to help the folks across the city. And Cokie said, Donna, they've got all of these wonderful frames made out of wood from the Ninth Ward where the houses got flooded out, grab some of that, that's going to be worth something. So I went and got them. The first thing I did, I said, girl, we'll put your picture in this damn frame so that I'll always remember that you were the one who told me to treasure everything that came from the city. She's on my mantelpiece with my mom and a lot of other great people. I wanted her there with Shirley Chisholm and Coretta Scott King. I got Barbara Jordan and I also have Maya Angelou because Cokie's in the sisterhood. She's with the sisterhood up there. But more importantly, she was a member of the family. She was a member of the colored girls society. Cokie could talk to you like she was Black too. I would sometimes forget that Cokie was white, I just forgot, I really truly forgot. She understood us. She had our stories written in her own voice. She included us in her story. And so she belongs on that mantelpiece. She belongs as part of that group of women that inspired me, who mentored me, but who pushed me. And that's why she's there."

Amna Nawaz

In Amna Nawaz's family, books were "a really special gift," and she remembers getting a copy of Cokie's first book, *We Are Our Mothers' Daughters*, from her parents: "She was an example for us. My parents were immigrants to this country from Pakistan. So my sisters and I are first generation American and my parents were very intent on putting before us examples of the kinds of things that you can do and the people that you can be. It was, look at this incredible woman, look at everything she has accomplished and look at the person that she is and the work that she does and the difference that she makes. This is a path that you can take. It wasn't something they explicitly said, but I realize now looking back, that's what they were doing."

When Amna started at ABC she was working for a new digital service, the "JV team," as she put it, and one day she headed for the makeup room before going on the air: "I was walking by the room about to pop in as I normally did and Cokie was sitting in one of the two chairs. I briefly stopped in the door and then I just kept walking right by because I am not going in the room when Cokie Roberts is in that room. So I ducked around the corner and waited and thought, I'll just hang here for a bit. But I was going to be late, so I kind of gingerly poked my head in and said, I'm so sorry. Do you mind if I join you, and she immediately looked over and said, oh no, come on in! As if we were old pals. And so the makeup artist got to work on me and I said, Cokie, I don't want to bother you if you're getting ready for something. But I just wanted to say hi, I'm Amna, I just started here, and I'll never forget, the first thing she said to me was, oh yeah, of course I know who you are, and started chatting with me about the work that I'd been doing. And I was so taken aback because I never thought anyone like Cokie Roberts would be paying attention to what I was doing, like not in a million years. Feedback is such a weird and rare thing in TV news anyway, so to hear from Cokie Roberts that I was doing a great job—I mean I was basically walking on clouds the rest of the day."

Annie Whitworth Downing

As Martha Walters noted, Cokie was a "master matchmaker," and Annie, who was then Cokie's assistant at ABC, remembers: "It's funny because I went on a trip to New Orleans with Ward just as friends and I came back and told her, I think I kind of like him and she said, of course you do, because we'd been friends from college and she had met him before. So yes, she knows immediately when someone's bad for you and when someone's good for you." After Annie and Ward got engaged, Cokie went with her to pick out wedding invitations: "During lunch, we went to a Crane's store, within walking distance of ABC and she's like, here's the invitation you're going to get, here's what it's going to say. I'm obviously not from Louisiana, but I am from a Southern state and there are certain rules and etiquette and she knew what would be the perfect simple invitation." Then Cokie flew to Laredo, Texas, for the wedding: "She came the night before and we spent the whole day together. I have pictures of us getting dressed together. I remember she sat at my parents' table and my parents loved it." As a new bride she sought out Cokie for advice: "She was like a mother to me because I was far from home and I always went to her for relationship advice. One time I told her I was so frustrated because Ward couldn't do something around the house. And she said to me, Annie, you cannot make a handyman. If he is not a handyman, he will never be a handyman. And to this day I cannot forget that she told me that because she was so right." After Annie's first child was born, Cokie kept bugging her to bring the baby to work: "I said, I am not bringing my child to work, but Cokie would say, she'll be fine, I'll hold her. A couple of times I took Avery to work and Cokie would just hold her and be on the computer or have her in her arms, doing things. I can picture her sitting at her desk, baby in one hand, mouse in the other."

Ariane Naulty

The Boggs and Naulty families had known each other from New Orleans. Ariane attended the Sacred Heart school where Cokie's "picture was all over and everyone's like, she's our most famous alum. So when you're right out of college this person is like a movie star to you, right? They're larger than life." When Ariane went to work at ABC, "it was always my mom and my dad who were like, please, please follow Cokie. She's a good Catholic, just follow what Cokie does. She's from a good family. Also I looked up to someone like Cokie who was in a men's club and rose to the top and got there just by being smart and being tenacious and being persistent and being true to herself." One subject Cokie was "persistent" about was relationships. She pushed many couples together, but she was equally adamant when she thought a friend was making the wrong choice. And she minced no words with Ariane, whose boyfriend at the time belonged to Opus Dei, a very conservative Catholic organization: "Cokie was like, you need to break up with him, this is going to make your life miserable. So I was like, really? And she's like, oh God, Ariane, get rid of him now. I'd see her in the elevator, Sam [Donaldson] was there, or all these big executives and she'd be like, have you broken up with the Opus Dei yet?" Ariane followed Cokie's advice, dumped the guy, and married someone else: "Of course she was absolutely right. The guy was a total freak. I'm very glad I did not marry him. I was 20 years old, I had no idea what I was doing, but she was wise. I remember my mother addressing the invitations for our wedding and saying, thank the Lord you didn't marry the other one. I was like, why didn't you guys tell me this? Cokie was the only one who told me to break up with him."

Nina Totenberg

"I'm not sure how I would have survived the long illness and death of my first husband without Cokie," says Nina, Cokie's close friend for more than forty years. "If, on occasion, she heard my voice faltering on the phone, she would magically appear to bolster my spirits." Nina had married Floyd Haskell, a one-term senator from Colorado who was twenty-six years older. In January of 1994, he slipped on the ice in front of their house, severely injuring his head, and was rushed to the nearby hospital of Howard University. Cokie would visit regularly, and Nina describes her role: "The thing that she did that made her so special was she went to every doctor's conference with me that was important. So when we had a meeting with a doctor and a social services person, when they were going to send him home, she came with me and she took notes. And let me tell you, this was like in our union negotiations, she puts it in her notebook, it's there forever. And so when they didn't do something that they had promised, she would wave the red flag at them, and say, look, it's right here in my notes that you said somebody would come to the house in the morning to help get him ready for the day, and you're not providing that service. She was just relentless in keeping them to their word. It meant a lot that I had somebody with me. My mother was dead. My father wasn't very well going to come down and do this with me. I had a pal, a leader, a friend, somebody who loved me and who I loved and who was incredibly able and had been through this enough, I guess with other people, that she knew what to do. I didn't really know what to do."

A few years later, Haskell contracted lung cancer. Nina was in Oklahoma City doing a story for ABC's *Nightline* program when he hit a crisis, and Cokie went to Sibley Memorial Hospital to be with him. ABC arranged a charter flight to rush Nina home: "I get back and I go tearing over to Sibley and there's Cokie. She's sitting with him until I get there. And I think she possibly saved his life that day, because he was definitely circling the drain. And when I walked in the monitors all started to go up, the stats went up, everything went up. He smiled and he recovered and I think she kept him alive until I got there. And then she just left us. She gave me a big hug and she left." Floyd survived another year or two, and when he died in 1998, his body had to be transported back from Maine to Washington. Nina's memory: "I'd never been in charge of anybody who died, right? I didn't know how to do this and Cokie walked me through every step of the way. She ran Floyd's death. She told me what to do and I did it. I was like a semi-competent zombie and so she was the person in charge." One task was to pick out a casket, and they went together to the funeral home: "We were looking at caskets and I knew I wanted to spend the least money possible. Right? And so she and I are walking around and of course they're showing us every fancy casket in the world. Silver, gold, engraved, you can't imagine it. Finally we get to this little room that has their cheapest caskets, which were very beautiful, I have to say. And at that point I'm getting sort of worn down and I'm torn between two caskets. One is maybe $500 cheaper than the other, but the other looks prettier and has all kinds of blue silk lining in it. And the guy who was trying to sell us the caskets from the funeral home was the embodiment of the term 'obsequious.' He was tall, he had white, very white skin and black hair slicked back. I'm looking at these two caskets and I'm sort of undecided and he says to the two of us, 'You know, Ms. Totenberg, your husband was a very tall man and I think he'd be much more comfortable in this casket.' And the two of us turned away from each other because we were going to laugh out loud. We were just wracked with giggles, absolutely wracked with giggles. And you couldn't do that with everybody. You really couldn't. You just couldn't."

Eden Lipson and Margo Johnston

Eden Lipson was one of Cokie's oldest friends, a bridesmaid in our wedding, and not long after she was diagnosed with pancreatic cancer, she went into a potentially fatal spiral. Eden's daughter Margo: "Cokie called to check-in because she'd been checking throughout the day. And I stepped out to the waiting room and I said that's it. They told us to say goodbye. She's gone. Cokie said she can't be gone. There's no more trains. I don't know how she did it, but through some magical machinations, by taking some crazy middle of the night train, Cokie got to the hospital in New York at like three or four in the morning." Eden pulled through, but both women knew her time was short, and Cokie would travel to New York regularly to see her friend: "She was such a relief to Eden. Cokie would visit and they could sit and chitchat with their needlepoint and laugh about everything and nothing. What a comfort that was. They could jump between the most profound existential questions—how do you face death?—to thinking about recipes and holidays and how we mark time and ritual. Everything and nothing all at once. Sometimes you need your friends to give you permission to admit how bad and hard it is, and Cokie was one of very few people that Eden could do that with."

Eden's husband died a year after she did, so when Margo married her wife, Leanne, she had no parents left. Cokie flew to Pittsburgh, Leanne's hometown, and arrived just before the ceremony. Margo's memory: "There was this really wonderful and important moment when Cokie found me. She held my hands and looked at me, and for her and for Eden she was marking that moment. She told me my mother would have loved to be there. She told me my mother would be so happy and how happy she was that she could be there with me. Cokie was really the only person who could stand in for my mother, who could speak to that moment in that way."

Harriett Cunningham Plowden

I met Bob Plowden, a retired air force general, on the tennis courts at Pawleys Island, and our wives became fast friends. When Cokie learned that Harriett's mother, Mary Cunningham, was over one hundred years old and living just a few hours away in their hometown of Sumter, she insisted on meeting her. Harriett's memory: "She went with me probably four times to see Mother. First time, I can't remember how old Mother was then, she was probably 101 or 102 and so we got ready to leave and Mother stood up, took Cokie's hands in hers and said, Cokie, now you can tell me, are you a Republican or a Democrat? And Cokie looked her right in the eye and said, I'm a journalist. We took a picture that day and Mother still has it in her room." Mrs. Cunningham was a big Democrat herself and during the 2016 presidential campaign, when Hillary Clinton was due to make a stop in Sumter, Cokie decided they had to meet. Harriett's memory: "Cokie called me that morning and she said, I found out that Hillary is going to be in Sumter for a rally this afternoon. Would your mother like to go? Cokie called back about 3:30 and said they're leaving Columbia now and they'll pick your mother up and take her to the rally. Well, I call Mother and explained everything to her and she said, oh my gosh, I've got to go have my hair combed. So she called the man downstairs, they have a beauty shop in the building, and he combed her hair. They picked Mother up, took her out to Morris College (where the rally was held) and she had about 10 minutes or so with Hillary by herself, which meant so much to her. And then during the rally, Hillary introduced Mother to the crowd and said, this lady is 103 years old and she has voted in every election and I want you all to follow her. And Mother was just thrilled." As Mrs. Cunningham's memory started to fail, Harriett would complain to Cokie: "I was just kind of whining about it and Cokie said, two words, that's all you have to remember, be kind. So I spread those words to all my sisters and nieces and nephews and everybody. Just be kind and that's it."

Harriett's husband, Bob, was in declining health, and when he took a turn for the worse on a Sunday, he was rushed to a hospital in Charleston. Cokie called Harriett that Wednesday: "She said, I can come tomorrow or Friday. And I replied, I think tomorrow, because I knew we weren't going to be able to keep him alive much longer." She got the first plane out the next morning and went straight from the airport to the hospital. When the doctors said there was no longer any hope, Harriett told them to remove her husband from life support and Cokie stood with her friend at Bob's bedside as he peacefully died. Harriett continues: "Cokie came home with me, she canceled her car, she canceled her airplane reservation. She was going back that afternoon but she came home with me. I had been sleeping on the floor and on a chair since Sunday, so I was tired, but I didn't think I'd be able to sleep. Cokie put her arms around me and said, would you like for me to sleep with you? And I said, I don't think so, but it was like having my sister there. She was my sister in so many ways. In fact, that's how my sisters refer to Cokie, as our other sister."

CHAPTER SIX

Storyteller

*"History looks very, very different when
you see it through the eyes of women."*

If Cokie became a journalist by accident, the same could be said for her success as a book-writing storyteller. But in another sense, she had been training for that role her whole life. She never aspired to writing books, and as her visibility on television grew through the 1990s, and a publisher approached her about writing a memoir, she turned them down. Talk to my mother, Cokie told them—"She has a real story." When Cokie's first book, *We Are*

Our Mothers' Daughters, was published in 1998, she was already fifty-four years old. And when it stayed on the bestseller list for twenty-six weeks, including one week at number one, "she was absolutely floored, she could not believe it," says Claire Wachtel, her longtime editor. Yet looking back, Cokie's midlife career path should not have "floored" anybody. She was deeply proud of her own family's history in America, which began in 1621, when her ancestor William Claiborne landed at Jamestown. Ten years later, he sailed up the Chesapeake Bay and became the first white settler to step foot on what is today the state of Maryland. His descendants have served in public office in virtually every generation since then, and as she told radio interviewer Jill Ditmire, "I obviously do like to read history. At one point, actually, before I had ever written a book, I said to Steve, 'What I really want to do is just sit around and read history.' And he said, 'Nobody's going to pay you to do that.' And he was wrong, but I had to write it as well as read it, and the second part is a little harder."

"A little harder" is a huge understatement. Cokie had so many other obligations, professional and personal, that finding time to write was always a painful struggle. Faced with a crushing deadline, she found herself googling symptoms of a heart attack in women. Yet she eventually published six books (two coauthored with me) and turned two of her history books into children's versions. In 2018, when asked to name her "proudest achievement," she replied, "My proudest career achievements are the books. The books are very hard to do, and I think they're quite good frankly. And they are much harder than journalism." The two books we wrote together focus mainly on our interfaith relationship, but the other four are knit together by a strong simple theme: rescuing, reviving, and recognizing the contributions women have made to American history. As she told one interviewer: "One of the reasons I have been writing books about women in history is because other people haven't been. And telling history without talking about one half of the human race seems to me to be an inaccurate way of telling the story." To Steve Inskeep on NPR, she added: "It's terrible for any young person, but particularly a girl, to grow up thinking that women were not making tremendous contributions to the founding of the country and the continuation of the country." And while she focused her attention on women and girls, they were not her only target audience. "People say to me all the time, what's important for girls? But you know it's important for boys too," she said on C-SPAN. "I mean the notion that only girls can read about women just makes me nuts."

I often said that Cokie had a "mission" as a book writer, and she agreed with that description: "History looks very, very different when you see it through the eyes of women, and I would argue that the view is much broader, not only because it includes the other half of the human race, but also because the men become three-dimensional. When they correspond with the women they talk truthfully and especially when the women correspond about the men, instead of marble and bronze deities, the men we know as the founding fathers become flesh and blood, they're human beings. They are fathers, husbands, lovers, sons and friends with all the passion and playfulness and the flaws and feelings that go with those roles."

You might say that Cokie's book-writing career started with a clock radio. "She was always an icon to me," says her editor Claire Wachtel. "Every morning I would wake up to Cokie Roberts on NPR." So after Cokie initially rejected the idea of writing a book, Claire turned to her mother and engaged a writer to work with Lindy on a memoir. When the first draft came in, however, Cokie was dismayed. The writer, she complained, "hasn't captured my mother's voice," and at the last minute, Cokie revised the manuscript herself. The result, *Washington Through a Purple Veil*, was published in 1994 to generally favorable reviews, but it suffered from one major flaw. As a professional politician and purebred Southern lady, my mother-in-law was largely incapable of either criticism or candor. As she often remarked, "Darlin', imagine the book I could have written if I'd told the truth." Still, the experience of revising her mother's book had a big impact on Cokie, as Claire recalls: "She had never written a book before. She didn't know what a heavy undertaking it would be. And I think that helping Lindy write the book and rewrite it, sort of pushed her to do her own book. I think she saw that she had something to say."

Actually, Cokie had a lot to say. One goal of her first book was to document the experiences of her generation, women who had come of age in the early '60s and overcome enormous obstacles to professional success. The first female to appear regularly on a Sunday-morning TV show knew what she was talking about when she wrote in the introduction to *We Are Our Mothers'*

Daughters: "We were the pioneers—or so we thought. And in many ways, we were. We were the first women at almost everything we did, and most of us often had the experience of being the only woman in the room." Another goal was to say to those pioneers, pay attention to the past, don't forget the roles women have always played. When you're the only woman in the room, remember what happens when there are *only* women around. "Over the decades, as I witnessed and participated in this great social movement of the century, I had only one fear for women: that we would lose our sense of perspective," she wrote. "Our great strength in my view has been our ability to see beyond the concerns of the day. As the nurturers, the caregivers, we have always worried about the future—what it will mean for the children—and as the custodians and carriers of the culture, we've carefully kept alive the past. I was afraid that we might become so involved in the daily demands of the world of work that we would break the thread of connection to generations of women before us."

That's how she organized the book. Half the chapters were about women succeeding in "the world of work" as politicians and soldiers, mechanics and enterprisers. And half were about women as the "custodians and carriers of the culture," as wives and mothers, sisters and aunts. To Cokie, these roles were not in conflict; they were both critical to her view of the world. She was a radical and a traditionalist, a devoted feminist who deeply believed that true feminism meant expanding the choices available to women, not dictating what those choices should be in the name of ideological purity. She denounced her militant sisters who "engage in finger-pointing at women who make different choices than they do" and added: "I must admit that this often-vituperative argument about staying home versus going to work makes me nuts. It's not men who are doing this to women, it's women who are doing it to each other, trying to validate the decisions they make by denigrating the decisions of others."

As Claire said, Cokie didn't quite realize what a "heavy undertaking" even a modest book would be, and as usual she pushed the deadline to the limit. At one point she showed me a draft of the "wife" chapter and asked my opinion. After many years of working together, Cokie and I had learned to edit each other gently. So I said, with considerable apprehension, "Do you want a real edit? I want to know the ground rules here." Somewhat brusquely, she replied, "I don't have time to screw around, Steven, I need to know what you really think." When I read the chapter, I saw that she had written it too quickly; it lacked her usual bounce and flair. So I summoned all my courage and told her so. To my vast relief she replied, "I just read it over, and I agree with you." She also had trouble with the title. She had such a strong relationship with Lindy, as she told Charlie Rose on PBS, that "I desperately want to be my mother's daughter." However, she added, "I discovered it was a somewhat problematic title after I named it that because there are women who go running and screaming away from it." Or as one young editor at the publishing house told her, "I am not my mother's daughter. You can't make me be my mother's daughter."

Still, the book did so well because it touched so many nerves in so many readers. Women would tell her that after reading it, "I've called my mother for the first time in years." Claire Wachtel put it this way: "I think the book worked because she could speak to every woman. It was not polemical, it was not ideological, it was by example. Women could relate to that, and to who she was, a mother, a wife. She also walked the walk. She wasn't full of it." The book had the same impact and appeal as her appearances on television. The women who bought it and read it and gave it to their friends and daughters were the same women who had said years earlier, "I'm watching ABC more because when Cokie's on she always speaks up and says what I'm thinking."

Cokie's second book grew out of a feature that *USA Weekend* magazine published on Easter Sunday of 1997. We both wrote letters to our children, reflecting on how we had reconciled our mixed religious heritage, and Claire suggested we expand on that idea. Many couples find collaboration a perilous enterprise, but we had always enjoyed the experience and eagerly accepted the proposal. (Although we did agree to bank our entire advance, so if we hated the whole process we could easily quit and return the money.) We were summoned to New York for a fancy photo shoot to produce a cover image, and instructed to bring six changes of clothes each—different colors, textures, styles. It was all rather bizarre, made considerably more stressful by the fact that on the day of the shoot we had not written a single word of the book. When we finally did start writing, we hit a roadblock. We couldn't tell the story of our marriage in a single voice because we kept disagreeing on key points. So we turned to plan B, we'd each write separate chapters, but that didn't work either. If Cokie was describing our wedding on page thirty-two and I was discussing the same event on page fifty-five, we'd only confuse the reader. During this time I was occasionally hosting *The Diane Rehm Show* on NPR, and one day I interviewed a father and daughter who had written a book about their religious faith and told it in dialogue form. Bingo! Plan C! We pilfered their idea and hired a former student of mine, who was home with a new baby, to come to the house and ask us questions. We'd tape the answers and edit the transcript, a process that had two big advantages. We could do it quickly, and the conversational style kept the tone from being too stiff and serious. Cokie interrupted and corrected me frequently—after all, she had been doing that for years with David, Sam, and George—and we kept all of that dialogue in the actual book. We also decided to include stories of other marriages, past and present, and dividing the responsibility was easy. I favored living subjects, people you could actually interview, and Cokie always preferred to write about historical figures. As she later told C-SPAN, "It's really nice to write about dead people, they cannot argue with you."

Cokie's topics included marriages between slaves, immigrants, and pioneers, but what really engaged her was a portrait of John and Abigail Adams. In an interview with Bruce Cole of the National Endowment for the Humanities, she recalled her reaction: "When you cover Congress and politics as long as I have, you go back and read the debates on the right to bear arms, freedom of religion, those kinds of things, all the time. That period of history becomes a part of your everyday life. My ignorance of the women of the era astounded me. What do little girls learn in elementary school? Molly Pitcher on the battlefield or Martha Washington at Valley Forge, Dolley Madison saving George Washington's portrait, Betsy Ross and the flag. That's about it. So my ignorance was appalling. Then my husband, Steve, and I wrote a book on marriage called *From This Day Forward*, and included a chapter on John and Abigail Adams's marriage. I went back and started reading those letters, which are blessedly available, and I couldn't get over it. I couldn't get over her involvement in politics. I couldn't get over her influence on him and on other founders and I couldn't get over how alone she was for long periods of time and how brave she had to be and how, as she put it, how un-self-interested a patriot she was. As she said, 'I'm suffering all the hardships, making all the sacrifices for the cause, and I'm not going to get anything for it. I won't even be able to vote, but I am able to do this.'"

A seed had been planted, but it took some encouragement to sprout. After our marriage book appeared in 2000, and sold well, we assumed we'd write another one together, but we were still searching for a good topic when David McCullough published his mammoth biography of John Adams the next year. Cokie was furious, convinced that McCullough had not given sufficient credit to Abigail, and wrote a newspaper column saying so. She gave me the column to edit, and it was brilliant, passionate and powerful. I turned to her and said, "Honey, this is your next book." And so it was. It took Cokie another three years to produce *Founding*

Mothers, and in her introduction, she described the process: "As I read through the letters of John and Abigail Adams and became more and more fascinated with her life, I grew curious about the other women who had the ears of the Founding Fathers. These women lived through extraordinary times and must, it seemed to me, have extraordinary tales to tell. Now I know they do. It's safe to say that most of the men who wrote the Declaration of Independence and the Constitution, fought the Revolution, and formed the government couldn't have done it without the women. And it was the women who, insisting that the men come together for civilized conversation in the early Washington dinner parties, helped keep the fragile new country from falling into fatal partisan discord. The women made the men behave."

Her first idea was to start with Abigail Adams and the other women of the Revolutionary period and end with the presidency of Abigail's son John Quincy Adams in 1825. But she got too mesmerized by her material and, in typical fashion, risked missing her deadline. So the result was two separate volumes: *Founding Mothers*, published in 2004, which ended with the inauguration of John Adams in 1797; and *Ladies of Liberty*, published in 2008, which continued the story through John Quincy's tenure. Both books had a simple design: to retell the story of that period through a different prism, "through the eyes of women," and she used their own words, recorded in letters and journals and diaries, to do that. "With the exception of maybe five quotations in this book, every single one is written either by a woman, to a woman or about a woman," she said about *Ladies of Liberty*. "And that's very unusual in a history book."

Finding those writings proved to be very difficult. "Fortunately, some of the descendants of these women wrote books in the nineteenth century," Cokie told Bruce Cole. "They understood that the stories of the women of Revolutionary times were about to be lost, the people who had heard the stories were beginning to die out. A woman named Elizabeth Ellet went around and did interviews and collected letters and published a two-volume work in 1849 about the women of the Revolution." But the endemic sexism pervading the world of historic research meant that many of the institutions holding original documents relating to women didn't think they were important. So Cokie and her friend and assistant Ann Charnley had to do a lot of "detective work" to track them down and she described how they operated: "We would look in the footnotes of other books [for references to women] and trace back and call historical societies and see which ones were worth visiting. What you would find was that the historical societies, even if they have these women's letters, often had never transcribed them or had them in a box in a basement." The two sleuths had to do a lot of cajoling and convincing before these societies would take women's words seriously. One of them owned a valuable diary from 1793 and agreed to share it. And then sent a faxed copy in totally unreadable eighteenth-century handwriting. "There were things like that that happened all along the way," Cokie recalled. However, many of the curators in these places were women, and they were thrilled with Cokie's work and eventually signed on as her volunteer assistants: "After the first book, after *Founding Mothers*, it became easier because the people in the historic societies and the university libraries understood what I was up to and became more helpful. Since I've been doing these books, there has been a lot more recognition that women's letters are worth publishing. But once you finally find this stuff, it is very, very difficult to read. And so I actually have to hire people to decipher it. I can't read most of it."

Cokie insisted that the effort was worth it because "women's letters are really so much better than men's letters," as she told David Rubenstein for his book *The American Story*. The reason is that "the Founders knew that what they were doing was extraordinary. They were self-aware men, and they knew that if they failed, they'd be hanged, but if they succeeded, they would be held in acclaim, that their writings would be published, and they wrote with that in mind. I always joke that we see our Founders as bronze and marble statues, and their letters read like they were written by bronze and marble statues. They are edited, and they are considered, and they are in some cases pompous." The women's letters are exactly the opposite: candid, not considered; personal, not pompous: "The letters that the women write, where they have absolutely no expectation that we're going to be reading them two hundred years later, are just completely unvarnished, frank and real. You get a much more complete view of the society as a whole. So in the same sentence you might hear about how we really have to declare war against France, and so-and-so's pregnant again and it's scary because her last baby just died, and by the way, I need the bonnet I left at home. So you get a much fuller picture of society, and you also get a much truer sense of the men. I actually think we can admire the Founders more as flesh-and-blood people. Because it's easy for a deity to do something extraordinary, but for just a guy to do something extraordinary is hard. And that's what they were. They were guys."

Cokie was not a professional historian and never pretended to be one. She was not unveiling new theories or unearthing new secrets. She was a storyteller, and her stories contained two core lessons. One was that women were a civilizing—and essential—influence because they "made the men behave." Otherwise, the males of the species would revert to their more natural and nefarious instincts. The second lesson was that whatever great deeds men accomplished, they "couldn't have done it without the women," who were a constant source of counsel and consolation, encouragement and enlightenment. They were also witty. Cokie delighted in their sense of humor and loved telling the story of what happened one year when Congress stayed in session later than usual, and the lawmakers left behind forty pregnant and unmarried women. Louisa Catherine Adams, John Quincy's wife, wrote to her father-in-law, John Adams: "I recommended a petition to Congress next session for that great and moral body to establish a foundling institution and should certainly move that the two additional dollars a day, which they have given themselves as an increase in pay, may be appropriated as a fund toward the support of the institution." She would laugh every time she recounted that tale and add, "Now, it doesn't get any better than that. And you can be sure you have not read this in any book by a guy historian." She often quoted Martha Washington, who wrote to a niece, "I really think of myself as the chief state prisoner." In fact, when Cokie interviewed Laura Bush and Michelle Obama together in 2013, she repeated Martha's observation and asked if the two First Ladies felt the same way. "No, no, there are prison elements, but it's a really nice prison," replied Mrs. Obama. "But with a chef," chimed in Mrs. Bush.

Cokie never hid her affection or admiration for her subjects, and she became something of an evangelist, preaching the gospel of their significance. She did extensive tours to promote her books and spoke often around the country at various symposiums and seminars. "She loved these women she wrote about," said Dee Dee DeBartlo, her longtime publicist. "It always seemed like she was friends with these women. She loved their backstories. She loved their gossip. She loved reading their letters." Her audiences, on the page and in person, sensed her exuberance, but she was also making a larger point: appreciate what women have always done—and what you can do too. "Cokie loved really getting at the humanity of these women, and she loved the fact that they were power players in their own right," said Dee Dee, who heard her speak many times. "And that would really excite and empower the women in her audience." One group she particularly enjoyed talking to were history teachers, since most of them were women and would go home and spread the good word to their students. Nancy Hayward, who ran the program that brought teachers to Mt. Vernon, and then distributed the sessions online, said, "If it was a program that Cokie was leading or was part of the panel, our viewership went up tremendously. It wasn't just because of what she was talking about. It was the way she talked to people. It was the way she brought you into that story and her enthusiasm for it. It may sound strange to say, but Cokie was a heroic figure to many of us who worked in museums, particularly in education museums because she just didn't say no. To me, history is just stories. And her books expanded the field of whose stories were being told, and made you want more." She also "expanded the field" of who would hear those stories by writing her two children's books, and this talk at USC conveys the absolute glee she felt at reaching young audiences: "The children's book of *Founding Mothers* came out last year, with fabulous illustrations by the incredible Diane Goode, and so I went around talking to kids about it. And I would say to them, you know all those pictures of the Declaration of Independence and the Constitution, was anything missing? And the little boys would always say something completely outlandish and weird. But the little girls—finally, finally—one of them would raise her hand and say, women. There are no women in the pictures. And I'd say, right, well, do you think there were women then? And they'd get all giggly, you know, because there were women then. And I'd say, how do you know? Well, that leads to sex, frankly. And that was tough on them at age eight, but then they would say, well, you know, there couldn't be men without women. Bingo!"

Yes, she "seemed like she was friends" with Abigail and Martha and Dolley, but her connection was even deeper than that. "I think that Cokie saw herself in a lot of these women," said Dee Dee, and occasionally she would make the comparison directly. One favorite character was a journalist named Anne Newport Royall, and as Cokie told students at the University of Southern California, "she was actually arrested, the first North American ever to be arrested for the crime of being a common scold." The woman who tangled on television with the likes of John Tower, Ross Perot, and Bill Clinton added mischievously, "Now, honestly, were it still a crime, I would be in deep, deep trouble."

Her regard for the historical figures she wrote about was matched by a certain disdain for modern women who, in her view, complained too much about their lot in life. "I've learned that women throughout our history have been incredibly influential and unbelievably brave and terribly smart and that modern women are basically sissies," she told one somewhat shocked interviewer. Cokie could be pretty judgmental at times, and she expanded on her point with Charlie Rose: "They think they're the first generation to have to keep all these balls in the air. They worry about the children. They worry about the job. They worry about all these things. And I had the great advantage of growing up with my mother, who always did everything, and who taught me that women always had. That the women who came across the ocean to this country or the women who trekked across the plains to settle the West were doing an incredible number of things at the same time, and as far as we know they weren't complaining that they couldn't 'do it all.'"

She could be even more critical of the men in her books, especially those who treated their wives badly. "I really get to the point where I lose all patience with the men," she told Rubenstein. John Adams, for example, "did do really stupid things," she fumed: "Think about this. So, he's in France, right? She [Abigail] is in Braintree, Massachusetts, trying desperately to keep body and soul together. She's suffering tremendously . . . She's got these four little kids. She's taking care of the parents, and there are periods when there really isn't enough to eat and all that. And he writes to her about how wonderful the women in France are. I mean, this is death time." She was often asked what woman should replace Alexander Hamilton on the ten-dollar bill, and Clara Barton, founder of the Red Cross, was her usual answer. Due to the huge success of the Broadway musical *Hamilton*, the first treasury secretary remains on the currency, but Cokie never missed a chance to express her disdain for him. "I've got absolutely no problem getting rid of Alexander Hamilton, not my favorite," she said on C-SPAN. "Cute, he's cute. I'll give him cute. But Alexander Hamilton not only cheated on his wife, he then fought this ridiculous duel, leaving her penniless with seven children. So if he was such a great secretary of the treasury, why was his wife left in debt?" And she loved this story about Martha Washington: "She named her tomcat Hamilton, which was most appropriate."

Her two history books both made the bestseller list, and Cokie assumed she would continue the saga chronologically, but she had trouble finding a theme that could match the vibrancy and significance of the Revolutionary period and its aftermath. She briefly considered, and rejected, the idea of writing a biography of Sarah Childress Polk, the wife of President James K. Polk, who served from 1845 to 1849. When her publisher suggested she write a book about the Civil War, to coincide with the 150th anniversary of the war's end in 2015, she was initially reluctant. As she told one interviewer: "My publisher really wanted a Civil War book, and I really didn't want to write a Civil War book. Partly because my ancestors fought on the wrong side, and partly because I hate the Civil War. It was such a failure of the political system, and I do believe in the political system, I think the founders had it right. And so the idea that they couldn't get to emancipation without killing a half a million Americans is just so depressing and wrong that I didn't want to deal with it, frankly. And also there are lots of Civil War books. But the publisher wanted one, so I sort of stalked around and tried to figure out what on earth this book would be. Obviously I knew it would be about women, but I didn't know what. I do think that the value added that I bring to history books is my political awareness, so that I can talk about the politics of the time in a way that you don't read in a lot of other history books, and so Washington was the obvious focus. And then once I started thinking along those lines, then it was, well, I wonder what the women were doing in Washington at the time. And did the war change the lives of women the way

World War II did? And did it change Washington the way World War II did?"

Cokie's reference is instructive. The Civil War was ancient history, but she had been born during World War II, and seen the lingering effects of that conflict during her childhood. At Washington's Politics and Prose bookstore she recalled: "And so I started thinking about my own growing up here after World War II. And the effects of the war were very physically present. The mall was covered with what were called temporary buildings. They had initially gone up in World War I and then more had been added in World War II. I remember asking my parents what 'temporary' meant because they didn't seem to be going anywhere. So you saw physically how the war had increased the government and made the city a bigger, more important city." That memory spurred and shaped her research: "So I started thinking, I wonder if the Civil War had a similar impact on the role of women, the place of women, and the role of Washington. And as I started to do the research, I found out absolutely and dramatically so. And so that's the book. Women started arriving in Washington just as they did in World War II mainly just to make a living because the men were gone. They needed a job. But then it was fortuitous for women. Just as they started showing up, Congress authorized the printing of paper money to pay for the war and the money comes off the machines in these great huge sheets. And of course, now the bills are cut up by machines, but then it required somebody sitting with a pair of scissors, cutting out each bill. And the treasurer of the United States said women are just better with scissors than men are. And he also allowed as how he could pay the women less, something that I've had several bosses say along the way in my career."

As that story indicates, digital technology had given Cokie access to a whole new source of information that was not available when she started writing books: newspapers of the period that she could easily read online. That enabled her to write about women who had not left letters and journals behind, including those scissor-wielding treasury workers and "a couple of dozen very young women who were killed in a horrible arsenal explosion." But her main focus remained well-educated and well-positioned women, and she was particularly struck by the fact that as war broke out, and Southerners fled the capital, female friends on both sides of the widening divide tried desperately to stay in touch with each other. Their stories symbolized one of Cokie's core beliefs, as she wrote in *We Are Our Mothers' Daughters*: "the great strength of women" is that "we are connected throughout time and regardless of place." One friendship that especially intrigued her was between Elizabeth Blair Lee, the daughter of a close advisor to President Lincoln, and Varina Howell Davis, the wife of Jefferson Davis, the president of the Confederacy. "These women would not let their friendships disappear even though the men were killing each other, because they had become so close," Cokie noted. She was particularly fond of Davis, who was "never fully accepted by the South" for two reasons: her grandfather had been governor of New Jersey and her complexion was too "tawny," as the Richmond papers put it, "to be a true

Southern belle." Cokie also relished Davis's sense of humor, and often quoted her reasoning for moving to New York after the war ended and her husband died: "So she wrote to her daughter and said, I am free brown and 62. I can move wherever I want." In New York, Davis befriended Julia Grant, the widow of Ulysses S. Grant, the general who had defeated the Confederacy. "When they first met, it was page one news in all the newspapers in the country," Cokie noted. "And then she [Davis] went to the dedication of the Grant Memorial very publicly, in a very considered act of reconciliation."

Dee Dee DeBartlo observed that Cokie "saw herself in a lot of these women" she had written about in an earlier period, and I think that was true of Varina Davis as well. She said "I hate the Civil War" in part because it highlighted a tension that ran down the center of her own family. Cokie embraced her family's rich heritage in Virginia and Louisiana over what is now four hundred years, and she could not ignore the fact that her great-great-uncle, William Robertson Boggs, was a Confederate general who didn't surrender until weeks after Robert E. Lee's capitulation to Grant at Appomattox. Her mother is buried in New Roads, Louisiana, next to Cokie's great-grandfather, Louis B. Claiborne, whose grave marker reads C.S.A., CONFEDERATE STATES OF AMERICA. But Cokie also shared her parents' fierce commitment to civil rights. Her father had been the only congressman from the Deep South to support the Voting Rights Act of 1965, and more than one cross had been burned on their lawn in New Orleans during her childhood. That's why, I believe, she was so struck by Varina

Davis's courageous "act of reconciliation" with Julia Grant. She could see herself doing the same thing.

Producing the Civil War book, *Capital Dames*, became a brutal and bruising experience. Her deadline was the end of 2014, so it could be published the next year, to coincide with celebrations marking the war's end. But three male relatives she cared deeply about—our brother-in-law Paul Sigmund; my twin brother, Marc Roberts; and her brother, Tommy Boggs—all died within a six-month period while she was trying to concentrate on the book, sapping her reserves of time and energy. "We had had a tough year last year in the family, so I was not finished with the book until February," she told one interviewer. "That meant spending January, getting up at three in the morning and just writing straight through till six or seven at night. So that was a rough month." To say the least. Claire Wachtel talked to Cokie about searching the web for heart attack symptoms and recalls: "I said to her, 'I think they're anxiety attacks. And you can hand it in late, who cares? It's not a book about a timely event. It's not time sensitive or anything. So we'll publish it a month later or a season later,' and she said, 'No, no, no, I can't do that. I have a commitment. And I have a date. And I have to do it.' And I said, 'You don't have to if it's going to kill you.' And she just insisted that she had to make that deadline." I remember Cokie asking Claire, "What's the real deadline? What's the absolute drop-dead date?" And she must have finished on the last possible day. Then she had perhaps two months before going on tour to promote the book, and during one interview she said, "People keep saying to me, what's your next book? And I keep saying, that's like saying, 'Mrs. Roberts, you just had triplets. When are you having another baby?'"

She never did write another book. She had contracted with her publisher to write a biography of Dora Lewis, a leading figure in the suffrage movement, to coincide with the one hundredth anniversary in 2020 of women gaining the right to vote. But two obstacles stood in her way. She never felt quite the same affection for Dora that she had lavished on the women in her earlier books, and as she had accurately noted, "the books are very hard to do." If you're not passionate about your subject, the task becomes almost impossible. Moreover, in the summer of 2016, just over a year after *Capital Dames* was published, she discovered that her breast cancer had returned after fourteen years. And that changed everything. There were periods of hope, when her medications seemed to be working, followed by periods of discouragement, when the drugs lost their effectiveness and she had to switch therapies. She said to me often, "If I knew I was going to be well, I'd do the book. If I knew I was going to be sick, I wouldn't. But I'm caught in the middle." She had similar conversations with Claire: "She called me up one day and said, 'I have to decide whether I'm going to spend what might be the last year of my life writing this book, or with my family.' And I said, 'Your family.' But she says, 'Well, I made a commitment.' And I said, 'Screw the commitment. Who cares? You have a legacy. You have all these books, you're a bestselling author. What more do you have to do?' You know what she said? 'I don't want to disappoint you.'" That was pure Cokie. She never wanted to disappoint anybody and she never did. But the questions remain: Why did she become a historian? And what contribution did she make?

Start with the inspiration she drew from her own family's legacy. Towns and counties in four states—Maryland, Tennessee, Mississippi, and Louisiana—are named for her Claiborne ancestors. So was a fort in Alabama during the Creek Wars of 1813–14. Six years after W. C. C. Claiborne became the youngest person ever to sit in the House of Representatives, President Jefferson bought the Louisiana Territory from France and made him the first governor. The longest street in New Orleans is named for him. When author Steve Hess ranked American political dynasties in terms of prominence, he initially placed the Claibornes third behind the Roosevelts and Kennedys. But after Cokie discovered several relatives who had served in Congress that Hess had overlooked, she badgered him into revising his ratings and moving the Claibornes up to second place. Since her parents served in Congress for almost half a century, I often joke that we don't believe in term limits in our family, and the only room in the US Capitol named for a woman is the Lindy Claiborne Boggs Congressional Women's Reading Room.

But Cokie didn't just read history, she lived it. "My childhood home was filled with politicians my entire life," she wrote. "They were friends, courtesy 'uncles,' fascinating storytellers, dedicated public servants and a few genuine wackos. As children, my brother, sister and I thought of people like Sam Rayburn, Lyndon Johnson, Hubert Humphrey and Gerald Ford as family friends who came by for a casual dinner from the garden." She loved to tell this story about "Mr. Sam," then the Speaker of the House: "The dog ate my pet chicken. And we were having a burial, and my brother started singing 'Dragnet' at the burial. Sam Rayburn had shown up, which he would do. He would just show up. I went running inside, sobbing, because my brother was singing 'Dragnet' at the chicken's funeral. And 'Mr. Sam' came out and sang, 'Just a Closer Walk with Thee.' The chicken had a proper burial." The Boggs children were always included in those dinners, Cokie recalled for *Southern Living* magazine: "What my parents decided when we were small is that if we were to have all the disadvantages of a political family, we should have the advantages. We were never shut away. When fancy people would come, we were invited too. We were included in all the conversations. And if a good piece of legislation would be on the floor, we could take the day off from school and go to the Capitol and watch." She knew politics from the ground up and the inside out. As a child, she told *TV Guide*, she thought that the Capitol "just happened to be where Daddy worked." Since House members run every two years, the campaigning was constant, and as Cokie wrote, "I loved stuffing envelopes at our dining room table with the campaign volunteers; it made me feel wonderfully competent to be able to fold the election flyers with the best of them." When she was sixteen, she was queen of the annual Mardi Gras Ball in Washington and the subject of a cover profile in the *Washington Star* newspaper. She told the author that she hoped for a career in politics and loved campaigning: "I can't stay away.

When election day comes around, I feel as though I'm supposed to be at the polls."

In later years, however, when she was asked about why she wrote history books, she usually mentioned her mother, not her father. At the 92nd Street Y in New York she said, "The main inspiration that I have had for all of these books was my mother, Lindy Boggs, who was a congressional wife for many decades." She elaborated at Politics and Prose: "When I was growing up here, in post–World War II Washington, I watched the women, my mother and her cohorts, running everything. They ran the political conventions. They ran the voter registration drives. They ran their husbands' campaigns. They ran their offices. And along with the African American women in Washington, they ran all the social service agencies. In fact, when my father was killed in a plane crash and my mother then ran for Congress, she called Lady Bird Johnson, who was one of her closest, closest friends and one of this group of remarkable women. And she told her that she was going to run for Congress and didn't want Mrs. Johnson to read it in the paper. And Lady Bird said, 'Well, that's nice, Lindy, but how are you going to do it without a wife?'"

When Cokie started researching the "founding mothers," she recognized them immediately because she had seen her mother and "her cohorts"—Lady Bird Johnson, Pauline Gore, Betty Ford, and many others—playing very similar roles. Cokie was particularly fascinated by the parallel between Lindy and Dolley Madison, who was absolutely critical to her husband's political success. "She actually reminds me a lot of my mother," Cokie once said of Dolley, and she loved to quote Charles Cotesworth Pinckney, the man James Madison defeated for the presidency in 1808: "I ran against Mr. and Mrs. Madison. Had I just run against Mr. Madison I might have won." At the heart of Dolley's—and Lindy's—political talent was the ability to transcend partisanship and temper rivalries, to form friendships and alliances that eluded their less diplomatic husbands. Cokie often told this story: "Henry Clay said to Dolley at one point, 'You know everybody loves Mrs. Madison.' And she said, 'That's because Mrs. Madison loves everybody.' Now I have read her mail. I know that's not true. But that was the effect she had, and really, the other women who came with her and after her kept that spirit of comity going." Lindy Boggs certainly had the same effect, and that's why, after Hale's death, she was elected to Congress nine times by overwhelming margins. But there was one problem. Lindy, like Dolley, had prospered because both women seemed to "love everybody" and had few enemies. When Lindy entered Congress, however, when she stepped from backstage into the spotlight, she had to vote, and finally reveal how she really felt on many issues. As Cokie's sister, Barbara, used to chide Lindy, "There's no 'maybe' button, Mama." Cokie credits her mother in another way as well. "My mother was a great historian, and she's the person who really imbued a love of history in me," Cokie told C-SPAN. "She was the chairman of the bicentennial of Congress. She had been chairman of several bicentennials along the way. And my sister said to her, you know, Mom, this is a great gig. Everything's likely to turn 200 at some point."

Cokie often offered another explanation for her book-writing bent. "Journalism led me to history," she told Charlie Rose, and elaborated in *Louisiana Cultural Vistas* magazine: "Because I cover congressional politics, I've had to spend a lot of time with the Founding Fathers—I know them all by first name—because if you're going to write about questions like the right to bear arms or religion in the public square, things that have become constitutional questions, you need to go back and see what they said. When people say 'the Founders said,' you need to know whether they are telling the truth or not. So I spent a great deal of time with the men and realized I knew nothing about the women. I started trying to find out about the women and realized that there really hadn't been much written about them at all, and that if I wanted to know about them, I'd have to do it myself. And once I found out about them, I decided I might as well write about it."

Her journalistic experience also sharpened Cokie's own feminist feelings. When her mother was elected in 1973, there were only sixteen female lawmakers. By the time she started covering Congress five years later, the number had barely increased, and Cokie made it a point in her reporting to document the contributions those women were making, often in a bipartisan fashion. She frequently told the story of what happened to Lindy after her father's death: "She found that she had the experience of a great many women, which was that not only did she lose her husband, but she lost her credit. And she got to Congress and she was on the banking and currency committee, a good place to fix this. And as she tells the story, they were writing a bill that ended discrimination in lending. And it said on the basis of race, religion, or national origin. And she says, she went into a back room and wrote in longhand 'or sex or marital status' [on the draft legislation] and Xeroxed it and brought it in and said to her colleagues in her oh-so-sweet Southern way, 'You know, I'm sure this was just an omission on the part of my colleagues.' And that's how we got equal credit. It is something that has happened on issue after issue, where women bring their own experiences to the table, and the experiences of women all over the country that come to them and tell them." Cokie often emphasized that modern women—like their historical sisters—worked across party lines more easily than their male counterparts, especially on issues relating to gender. In an oral history interview, she recounted what happened to Bobbi Fiedler, a conservative Republican who was elected from California in 1980 and appointed to the Budget Committee: "And so the Budget Committee is meeting, and there was something that they were zeroing out about women in science. She said, 'Wait a minute. Stop. Don't do that. We can't get rid of that.' And they said, 'What are you talking about? You're supposed to be the big fiscal hawk here.' She said, 'Look around the room.' And still they didn't get it. And finally she said, 'I'm the only woman in the room. And if I don't protect this program—which I have learned, since I've been here, is a very valuable program—then nobody else will.' That role is, generally, embraced by women in Congress and sometimes to their surprise." Cokie admired lawmakers like Fiedler, who represented women's interests, and as a journalist she tried to do the same thing. That's why she always asked more questions about funding for mammograms than for MX missiles. Moreover, it infuriated her that women who ran for public office still faced enormous prejudice: "Look, there are still questions. You know, 'Who's going to take care of the children?' Now, this particular one drives me up a wall. There has never, ever, ever, ever, ever, ever, ever been a man running for Congress who's been asked, 'Who's going to take care of the children?' And most of them are, in fact, dads. [But] it is something that is commonly still asked of women."

Catherine Allgor, who wrote a biography of Dolley Madison and now heads the Massachusetts Historical Society, sees a direct connection between Cokie's journalism and her history books. When I asked her what motivated Cokie to write those books, she quickly stated: "A sense of outrage." Outrage against what? "Against the sexism of the world that we live in," Allgor replied. "She was arguing the case for her women that we take their words and their work and their lives seriously." "Outrage" is the right word. Cokie was her mother's daughter in many ways, but she was much more willing to say publicly what she really thought. While Lindy was reluctant to tell "the truth" in her own book, Cokie was never timid, and as she got older, she got even more outspoken—if that's possible. Sometimes her outrage took the form of sarcasm. She spent a lot of time at the National Archives, where the nation's most cherished documents are displayed in the rotunda, and encircling the ceiling of that room is a colorful mural depicting the deliberations of the Founding Fathers.

David Ferriero, the archivist of the United States, recalls: "Every time the two of us were in the rotunda . . . she would look up and remind me—as if I needed reminding—that there are no women in those murals, they're all white men." Indeed, Cokie was so persistent on the subject that Ferriero arranged to have portraits of four "founding mothers" projected on the mural as a tribute to Cokie. The historian who insisted that Mt. Vernon add "and Martha" to their official signs would have been deeply pleased, but she died before the project was finished and never saw it. At other times Cokie's umbrage was unbounded. After the 2016 election, when she started doing her "Ask Cokie" segment on NPR's *Morning Edition*, host Steve Inskeep rather innocently mentioned that "the House of Representatives passed the 19th Amendment to the Constitution granting women the right to vote." Cokie immediately shot back: "No, no, no, no, no, no, no, no granting—no granting. We had the right to vote as American citizens. We didn't have to be granted it by some bunch of guys."

Cokie was not the first or only writer to focus on the role of women in American history, but she was probably the most popular and accessible. Max Byrd, a historical novelist who worked with Cokie to publish the letters of the nineteenth-century writer Clover Adams, described her contribution this way: "In a way Cokie was writing in the general context of academic historians, discovering forgotten or overlooked parts of the past, particularly the role of women and then the roles of minorities. So in that sense, she was part of that big wave. But the fact that she was not an academic historian, she was someone who was readable, made her a very prominent voice for that kind of change. Cokie's instincts for the right anecdote or the right touch really were novelistic, that's what sets her apart from the plodding academic historian. But she was very scrupulous about the facts and she corrected me more than once on things I got wrong." Susan Stein, the senior curator at Monticello, Thomas Jefferson's home, made a similar point: "She knew how to tell a great story. And I think that she brought that to her books and brought it to a much wider audience than any historian ever could. You know, historians speak to historians, their books are published by academic presses and Cokie's books were published by major publishers and received major attention. And I think that she became in a way, a spokesperson or spokeswoman for the historical scholarship that was going on at the time. Cokie was profoundly aware of inequality and inequity and the treatment of women and she waged a battle to correct that." She didn't just wage that battle in her books, but in many public appearances and private conversations that really amounted to a modern version of Abigail Adams's immortal adage: "Remember the Ladies." Holly Cowan Shulman, editor of the Dolley Madison papers at the University of Virginia, put it this way: "Very few of us had the visibility to make a difference on an institutional level at the NEH [National Endowment for the Humanities] or the Library of Congress or whatever. Our voices just don't get heard. But Cokie's voice got heard. And so for somebody who was devoted to understanding what the daily lives of these women meant, she's the mouthpiece. She's the person who could say it and somebody would hear it."

Today, interest in the historic role of women and minorities is far more widespread that it was when Cokie published her first book more than twenty years ago. Catherine Allgor says you can only understand Cokie's importance if you understand that context: "You may not believe this, or maybe you will believe it. I really have had colleagues who question whether women's history was real history. And if it was, was it important? What could it tell us that was at all interesting? When I was a full professor with a PhD from Yale, I had people questioning that. The biggest thing that Cokie did was she let Americans know that there was a history out there that they weren't aware of. And if that's sounding familiar to you, one of the hallmarks of this moment that we're in, where we're learning about Jim Crow and systemic racism and redlining, lots and lots of Americans are saying we weren't taught this history. We didn't know the history. Well, that history was happening in the academy but nobody knew it. And the same thing with Cokie. She gave Americans a gift, I don't want to say of an alternative history but I'll say an enlarged picture of history because the women were there. And she showed that having the women there changed the story."

CHAPTER SEVEN

Believer

"I'm Catholic like I breathe."

Cokie once said, "I'm Catholic like I breathe." Her faith formed a major part of her identity and her values, and she wanted people to know that. When an interviewer on NPR noted she had been "raised Catholic," Cokie shot back: "Very Catholic."

When a questioner at a speech asked, "What is your favorite Sunday-morning news show?" she answered, "Mass." News organizations tend to be very secular institutions, attracting few people of faith and even fewer who talk openly about their beliefs. So it mattered that Cokie went out of her way to tell a producer, just before her first appearance on ABC, "I go to church every Sunday." And even after she became a regular on the Sunday-morning program *This Week*, she always made time for worship. Her friend Carole Simpson recalls: "She would go off to church after *This Week*, she'd plop her straw hat on, her bonnet or whatever, and she'd go to St. Matthew's [the cathedral around the corner from the ABC offices, where her funeral Mass was held]. And this is a time when religion is not that popular with everybody, but she wore it proudly. It was important to her and she didn't care who knew she was Catholic or that she believed." She'd go to St. Matt's when the Mass times were convenient, but she actually preferred neighborhood churches, where she could see old friends and feel a sense of community. While she was a devoted Mass goer, however, she didn't always make it on time, and firmly believed that her devotion "counted" if she was present for the Eucharist, the core of the Catholic service. Our son, Lee, tells the story of Cokie meeting Bill Otis, the mayor of Pawleys Island, SC, the beach town where we have a vacation home. "I'll see you at Mass at 10:30," Bill told Cokie. "But Bill, Mass is at 10," she noted. "I know," replied Bill, who had Cokie figured out, "but I'll see *you* at 10:30."

Her faith flowed from her parents, especially her mother, the future ambassador to the Vatican. "It really did come out of a set of values that my parents strongly espoused, which relates to the Baltimore catechism question of 'Who is man? Man is in the image and likeness of God.' And they really believed that. Once you believe that, everything else flows from that," she once explained. The nuns who taught her also had an enormous influence. Until she left for college, Cokie always attended schools—Holy Rosary in New Orleans, Stone Ridge in Washington—run by the Religious of the Sacred Heart of Jesus, or RSCJs (initials derived from their original French name). When an interviewer suggested she had been "raised to some degree by the nuns," Cokie asserted: "Absolutely. And I still am in very close contact with the nuns who raised me and their successors—great, great women." During her funeral, to honor that relationship, the offertory "gifts" of wine and bread were brought to the altar by a delegation of RSCJs—all wearing bright red scarves. One nun, however, learned a painful lesson that other authority figures would encounter in later years: don't mess with Cokie when she has something to say. "Know what she did when she was 9? Bit a nun," reported the *Washington Post*. Despite a "deep vein of affection and reverence for ladies of the cloth, she chomped down on one when she was a third grader." Cokie's version: "She put her hand over my mouth. I didn't like that. Besides, she had chalk on her hand. I said, 'If you do that again, I'm going to bite you.' She did it again."

In its purest form the message of the nuns was clear and compelling: live your faith and do good in the world. Sister Claire

Pratt, who was at Stone Ridge a few years ahead of Cokie and became a Sacred Heart nun, expressed the order's credo this way: "Religion was not just some pious practice or something that we kept to ourselves or even ritualized on a weekly basis, but we needed to go out to others, we were sent out to others. I mean it was ingrained in us." Cokie's friend Mary Lou Kenny, who was also "raised by the nuns," said: "Everybody's heard that saying, those to whom most is given, most is expected. That's a great line, but the nuns live it, they believe it, and they teach it, they teach it to you at a very early age and over and over and they teach you how to live it, not just talk about it." Another Sacred Heart nun, Joan Magnetti, stressed that Cokie's faith "was not a namby-pamby 'Oh, whatever you want to do to me, God, I am your vessel' kind of thing. She had that rugged faith that just was like the mountain. It was there."

If the teachings of the nuns were important so was their gender. Stone Ridge was so central to Cokie's faith because it was a Catholic institution run by and for women. All her role models, the source of her deepest values, were not male priests or bishops or cardinals but other females. "It was all women, strong women who taught her to be a strong woman," says author Phyllis Theroux, an old family friend. "The nuns were better than the church, by 10 times, they were the real liberated women." Cokie made a similar argument in an interview with the *National Catholic Reporter*: "My mother always makes the point—she was educated by the Sisters of St. Joseph—that you are always exposed to women who are running everything. That is such a strong message. I didn't see them having power in the church, but I saw a sort of alternate universe where you could be very seriously Catholic and care deeply about the teachings of Jesus without being particularly concerned with the comings and goings in Rome." That's why Cokie dedicated her book *Founding Mothers* to "the RSCJs, who take girls seriously—a radical notion in the 1950s." Indeed, Cokie was so inspired by the Sacred Heart nuns that she briefly flirted with joining the order. "It was something that she probably seriously considered for about 10 minutes when she was 13 years old," notes her childhood friend Cinda Perlman. "Then we basically became adolescents and found boys kind of interesting."

Although she never became a nun, I'm happy to say, Cokie never lost her admiration for the sisters. They were her heroes and she seldom missed an opportunity to say so. During a speech at the Catholic Academy of Bridgeport in 2018, she focused on one of her favorite topics: the Ursuline nuns who arrived in New Orleans in 1727 and established schools not only for girls, but for Native Americans and free Blacks as well: "Think of how hard this was—the dangerous and endless voyage, the long black habits, the totally strange and unsettled land they now called home! But they soldiered on, seeing needs and filling them, despite the hardships." That same moral code defines the Boggs women: "seeing needs and filling them." Her prime paradigm, however, was St. Philippine Duchesne, the French nun who brought the Sacred Heart order to America in 1818 and battled constantly with the bishops to establish schools in frontier towns along the Mississippi River. Speaking to the Missouri Historical Society,

Cokie extolled "this feisty, independent woman who had to work so hard to make men do what she wanted them to do! And she kept at it and kept at it. I was inspired by her all my life." In an interview, Cokie expressed admiration for the way St. Philippine "was always pushing at the church. I think it's the stories of her doing it on her own terms that have kept me in the church. I understand that it is my church, not the hierarchy's." Would she make changes in the church? "Oh, I'd ordain women tomorrow, and it would change everything," Cokie responded. When the reporter asked what she would say to St. Philippine, given the chance today, her answer was swift: "I'd say to her, 'We need you back. Talk some sense into these people.'" That's vintage Cokie. She talked sense into people her whole life—especially powerful men, including those wearing Roman collars.

When nuns would invite Cokie to speak, she always accepted if she possibly could. On one notable occasion we both received honorary degrees from College Misericordia, a small women's school in Pennsylvania run by the Religious Sisters of Mercy. Since she always did her homework, Cokie googled the Sisters of Mercy but the reference that kept coming up was an Irish heavy metal rock band. Finally she found the right website, which reported proudly that several of the nuns had been arrested at a peace demonstration. And the judge in the case had sentenced the protesting sisters to forty hours of community service. Cokie giggled every time she told the story. Did the judge have a sense of humor? Or was he totally clueless? After the graduation ceremony we met informally with some of the sisters, and I quoted

Cokie's observation that as a child in Sacred Heart schools she had been taught, "The bishops are the pits!" One of the nuns then leaped out of her chair and gave me a high five. On another occasion her friend Sister Joan Magnetti asked a big favor: Mother Teresa was scheduled to be the graduation speaker at the Bridgeport Academy, but would Cokie set the date aside in case she had to pinch-hit? Two weeks before the ceremony, Mother Teresa fell in Rome and broke her ribs, so Cokie was summoned, Sister Magnetti recalls: "So of course I told the girls, they were fine, everybody understood and Cokie arrived, I'll never forget. She went out on the front lawn, looking drop-dead gorgeous, in a bright yellowy-orange dress and a big hat and she said, her arms outstretched, 'Clearly I am not Mother Teresa!'"

When Cokie was asked to join the board of the famous Mayo Clinic in Rochester, Minnesota, she was delighted to learn that a group of Franciscan nuns had helped create the organization in 1889, and irritated that the nuns were not given sufficient credit for their pioneering efforts. The clinic's website lists the two Mayo brothers, Charles and Will, as the official founders and deifies their memory, but Cokie was having none of it. It was the sisters, she insisted, led by Mother Alfred Moes, who first envisioned the hospital that later became Mayo, and when she gave the graduation speech at the clinic's medical school, she seized the chance to set the record straight. If you listen to her talk, you can hear the gasps of surprise in the audience as she delivered a classic Cokie rant: "Oh, yes. I know all about the marvelous Mayo brothers and their remarkable father, but had it not been for a pushy nun who wouldn't take no for an answer, St. Mary's Hospital would have never been built. And what became the Mayo Clinic might not have ever existed. Trust me, I know all about pushy nuns. I would not be here without them. I come from a line of great women who were shaped by the sisters." Whenever Cokie visited Rochester she tried to spend time with the surviving Franciscan sisters and constantly promoted their legacy. "I thought it was very important because for many, many, many years, the nuns never got credit," one of those Franciscans, Barbara Goergen, told me. "And when she got up to speak at those board dinners, it was always about us. She would speak about the nuns and that never happened before. We sat there with our little plates going, 'Yay, Cokie!' because it was something very new, very new. When you were with her, and I say this in all honesty, you felt, this is a holy woman."

While admiring sisters who stood up to male clerics—and physicians—Cokie had little use for the "namby-pamby" version, as Sister Magnetti described them. Ariane Naulty was Cokie's producer for several trips to Rome, covering major events in the Catholic church for ABC, and she recalls an assignment to find nuns "that were feeling liberated" and demanding greater rights. "So I found some nuns on the street and all the nuns were like, 'No, we love it, we love cleaning the floors, we love taking care of the priests,'" Ariane said. "And Cokie was like, 'I'm done with this piece. I'm not talking to any of these people. They're brainwashed and they're crazy.' And I was laughing so hard. I'm like, 'You don't think we can use any of it?' She's like, 'I'm not putting that on the air. These people, cleaning these men's toilets, making their beds, serving these men, no way. This is not what I want.'"

Cokie seldom missed a chance to tweak the male hierarchy of the church. "Now, does it make me furious, the patriarchy of the church? Absolutely," she once said. "And it makes me particularly furious on behalf of religious women because there they are doing this incredible work. I'm talking about nuns really doing the work of Jesus." Speaking in 2005 at Marquette University, a Jesuit school in Milwaukee, she began her remarks by saying, "I'm also really glad to be at a Jesuit event that I am not paying for, it doesn't happen very often." Then she noted that when her mother was appointed ambassador, she had been living in the French Quarter of New Orleans: "She moved from Bourbon Street to the Vatican and I teased her that the costumes didn't change. It was still guys in dresses, you know. In fact I was just back [in Rome] for the funeral of the Pope, with the Cardinals and all their petticoats. It's quite wonderful." One of her favorite riffs was to describe the American women who became saints, often after ferocious fights with their male bosses: Elizabeth Ann Seton, Katharine Drexel, Frances Cabrini. After telling those tales of female feistiness, Cokie would often comment acidly, as she did at one Stone Ridge graduation, "I'd like to point out these women are now canonized, they are saints. I don't know where the bishops they battled ended up for eternity, but their names don't show up in the litany."

Cokie struggled her whole life to stay faithful to an institution where women were relegated to second-class status and often said with some bitterness, "The nuns taught us we could grow up to become anything we wanted—except priests." As someone who cared so fervently about the welfare of children, the sex abuse scandals that surfaced in recent years only deepened her dismay with the male clergy. But she remained a devout Catholic simply because she wanted to. I heard her say many times, "It's my church. They can't run me out of it," and she refused to let the sins of the clerical fathers drive her away. She talked often with her friend Bob Murphy, who is gay, about their personal determination to stay loyal to a religion that treated them both so badly. "We both thought that our relationship with God and with Jesus trumped all of that other nonsense and how dare they try to interfere with our relationship, our personal relationship, with our faith," says Murphy. Mary Lou Kenny recalls Cokie saying that people who wonder why she remained a Catholic don't "understand what faith was all about." The source of true devotion, she added, "is not the altar, it's not the priest, it's not those kinds of things. It's the teachings of the church, it's the belief of the church and Cokie felt strongly and passionately about her belief in the teachings of the church."

From the earliest days of our relationship Cokie made it quite clear that I had to understand that passionate devotion to her religious heritage. My identity as a Jew was based mainly on tribal and traditional loyalties, not formal rites or rituals, and faith was a foreign concept in my family. Some of the nuns who had taught Cokie back at Stone Ridge had moved to Newton College of the Sacred Heart, a small women's school that later merged with Boston College, and one day she brought me to campus so the sisters could get a good look at her Jewish boyfriend. Apparently, I passed the test, but I still had a lot to learn. In January of 1966, eight months before we were married, she wrote me a three-page, single-spaced letter explaining what she could and could not do to reconcile our religious differences. She promised to strive "as much as humanly possible" to respect my feelings, and was "prepared to tell a weeping mother" that we would be married at home, not in a church building. "I know that we will love and be happy," she wrote. "Please, trust me to want that and to understand you well enough so that I will work together with you to that end." In turn she wanted me to understand her, to accept being married by a priest in a Catholic ceremony. "So it's not that emotionally I just can't stand to get married outside the church," she explained. "It's that I would no longer be a Catholic if I were not married by a priest. I know that thought galls you. I know you think it's an intolerant hierarchy and I must agree but that's the way it is and to ignore it is to divorce myself from it totally. That is not compromise and it is not something that I can do to either of us for the rest of our lives." As usual she was right. We both had to stay true to ourselves, otherwise the foundation of our marriage would be unstable from the outset. And our wedding became a test case for what we were trying to achieve: staying true to our own beliefs while embracing each other's traditions. I accepted the priest and the Catholic ceremony that was so basic to Cokie's faith. She agreed we'd be married at home, so my elderly grandfathers would not have to enter a church. There would be a chuppah in the garden, and a Jewish "elder" joining the priest. The compromise worked. A precedent had been set. We tried to follow that pattern of inclusion and respect for the rest of our married life.

The wedding was only the beginning of our journey together, however, the first of many adjustments and adaptations we would make over the next fifty-three years. "I think it would be easier to marry a Catholic, but that's not the way things worked out," Cokie wrote in her letter. "I have my doubts and my fears. I worry that the subject might be tense and awful, that we might both be plagued with guilt, that we might become defensive and try to prove the other wrong. But I don't believe that that is what will happen, first because we love each other too much, but also because we are aware of the problems and should be able to cope with most of them." Her prediction proved accurate. Wrestling with such a thorny decision so young gave us a template for surviving the rough patches that are inevitable in any marriage, and a confidence that conciliation was indeed possible. And Cokie set about keeping her promise, to do "as much as humanly possible" to make our interfaith relationship work. As a deeply devout person, she took all religions seriously, and embraced my Jewish heritage with joyful enthusiasm. When she became known as "the best Jew in the family," she joked that there "was not a lot of competition for the title," but she wore it proudly. In *From This Day Forward*, Cokie explained her motivation: "We realized that we had to create religious rituals for ourselves. Back home Steve knew that he was Jewish because it was simply part of the culture.

Now, if Judaism was going to be part of our marriage, we had to deal consciously with the religion itself. That was particularly true for me. I couldn't make any cultural claims to Judaism, so the religious rituals became terribly important to me."

One of those rituals was Chanukah, where we would light many candles on many menorahs so every child in attendance could have a chance to participate. Cokie was always fearful that we'd burn down the house—or at least singe a taper-wielding tyke—but it was my Catholic wife, of course, who made sure every youngster went home with a holiday gift. However, the Jewish ritual that became the center and symbol of our interfaith marriage was the Seder, the festive meal at Passover that celebrates the Jews' liberation from bondage in Egypt. The first year after our wedding we were invited to a Seder hosted by Justice Goldberg and his wife, Dorothy, and as Cokie recalled: "I was both mystified about what was going on and excited to be a small part of it. It wasn't until the crowd started singing freedom songs from the civil rights and labor movements, held over from the days when Goldberg had been a leading labor lawyer, that I felt I could participate with gusto." By the next year, when Cokie was pregnant with our first child, she decided we should have our own family Seder, and she asked my parents to host one. "They gamely said yes, though they had never held one before," Cokie recalled. "During dinner Steve's twin brother Marc called to talk to his folks and when their father said he would call back later because we were mid-Seder, we could all hear Marc's amazed, 'WHY?' at the other end of the line. We could also hear the whispered reply, 'Because Cokie wanted it.' Well, that was certainly true. And by the next year, after we had moved to California, where we knew hardly anyone, it was clear that if 'Cokie wanted it' she better figure out how to do it herself."

So she did, finding a Haggadah—the book containing the Seder service—at a local temple that had been published by the Jewish Reconstructionist Foundation in 1942. But after using it for one year, this child of the Sacred Heart nuns decided she could do a better job. As she liked to tell the story, she hauled out her battered old Smith Corona portable typewriter from college and patched together a more contemporary version, geared toward interfaith families like ours, from several different sources. "I also cooked a meal I was comfortable with—a Middle Eastern meal," she later wrote. "It seemed to me that the Bible was pretty clear about lamb being served on the night the angel passed over the Jews. No brisket of beef or boiled chicken ever made it into the book of Exodus. Also, these people were living in Egypt in springtime. I figured they had zucchini and okra and maybe eggplant. I knew for a fact that they had never met a matzoh ball. So I made my annual Middle Eastern Seder, and everyone made fun of me as a shiksa [a slightly derogatory term for a non-Jewish woman] who didn't know what she was doing. Thankfully, after a few years, the *New York Times* food section published a menu for a Sephardic Seder, a Passover meal for Jews of Mediterranean or North African extraction, and I was completely vindicated. Also the food was better. So our Seder quickly became somewhat famous."

During our California years many of our friends were like us, transplants from other places who were far from home, so our Seders acquired a special meaning, as a source of community and connection. They became so popular that when we left for Greece after five years on the West Coast, one of our going-away parties was a Seder celebrated a month early. When Passover did arrive, we were still living in a hotel in Athens, and knew absolutely no one, but the "best Jew in the family" insisted on holding a Seder, even if it was just the two of us plus Lee, age five, and Becca, who was three. She learned there was an old synagogue near the Acropolis and suggested I might find matzoh in the neighborhood, or at least pita bread, which was unleavened and could serve as a substitute. Now, I was new in my job, and taking myself much too seriously, so I completely forgot about my mission until the last moment. In a panic, I ducked into a pastry shop on the way home and bought some cheesecake. As Cokie told the story: "I said, 'What is this? We're having a Seder with a piece of cheesecake?' And Steve answered, 'Well, it's Jewish.'" Cokie, the keeper of the tablets, never quite forgave me for that one. But our Seders did flourish, as we gathered a new circle of families to celebrate with us. At a certain moment in the service the youngest child is sent to look for Elijah, a prophet said to be a messenger from God. Small children don't always understand the symbolism involved, and that Elijah never does show up, and as Cokie recalled: "One year, I guess it was our first real Seder in Greece, Lee asked, 'Daddy, when you were a little boy and both of your parents were Jewish, did Elijah come?' He thought Elijah was boycotting me, the shiksa."

Once we returned home, the Seders blossomed, getting bigger every year. Almost all the guests were in interfaith relationships, and some years my parents, who attended religiously, were the only two Jews married to each other. Back in California, we had printed out copies of Cokie's Haggadah using an ancient technology, a mimeograph machine, and those handmade documents served as the text for our Seders over the next twenty-five years, sanctified by loving care—and plenty of food and wine stains. Then friends decided we needed an upgrade, so Cokie eliminated the male-centric gender references and ran off a spiffy new version on a photocopier—without the blotches. Folks in the Jewish publishing world eventually heard about her text and suggested we publish it as a book, aimed primarily at interfaith families. We liked the idea, but after reading it over carefully, I thought it could use some modernizing. When Cokie saw my suggestions, she sternly informed me: "You can't change a word, this is sacred text." Now, I had not stayed happily married all those years by ignoring her more forceful opinions, so I complied. But then she started making her own edits. "You told me it was sacred text, that I couldn't change a word," I complained. "That's right," she replied, "I said that *you* couldn't change a word. But I wrote it, so I can." Eventually we reached a détente and a slightly revised version of Cokie's original effort was published in 2011 as *Our Haggadah: Uniting Traditions for Interfaith Families*. I've often joked that I was certainly the only Jewish guy from Bayonne, NJ, whose mother-in-law became ambassador to the Vatican. I'm pretty sure Cokie was the only daughter of an envoy to the Holy See who wrote a Passover Haggadah.

At a book talk after *Our Haggadah* was published, someone asked whether our individual faiths had been strengthened or diluted by a mixed marriage. "I would answer strengthened," Cokie replied. "I think that each of us has come to understand why our faith was important to us to begin with. And that was true when we were going through the conversations about getting married. Why were we having these agonizing conversations? Because it mattered. I think that not only have our own faiths been strengthened, but I think that we would both say that our lives have been greatly enriched by the other's faith." Yes, I would. I could never match Cokie's loving embrace of my heritage and become "the best Catholic" in the Boggs family, but I did come to appreciate how her fervent faith had produced many of the qualities I loved so much about her. And our life together gave me some insight into Catholic observances that "greatly enriched" my perspective. Perhaps the best example came during Lindy's time as ambassador. We were visiting her in Rome and got invited to attend a private Mass celebrated by Pope John Paul II at his summer retreat in the hills outside the city. As Cokie described the scene: "We walked into this tiny chapel and saw the sun shining on the aged Pope kneeling on a prie-dieu, a kneeler, in front of the altar, and we gasped because we felt we were in the presence of holiness."

"In all our married years together," Cokie once wrote, "not

one of the arguments that typically spice married life has been about religion." That's true, but in some ways, combining faiths was easier for us than it was for our children. As our son, Lee, often put it, "Each of you knew who you were. We were the experiments."

While we never argued between ourselves about religion, our embrace of an interfaith family did not always sit well with others, particularly observant Jews. While we were living in Greece, we took a trip to Israel with the kids, and I wrote an article for the *Times* about it. Letters poured in from my Hebrew brethren, who were outraged that I would marry a Christian, and dare to take my hybrid children to the Holy Land. But the most painful part was about my grandfather Abe Rogow. I wrote about his early years as a Zionist pioneer in Palestine, before he emigrated to America, and a number of readers essentially said, "Your poor sainted grandfather, how upset he would be if he were still alive to know that you had married outside the faith." To this day, I am enraged by that response. In his declining years, Abe seldom recognized his own children but would ask for Cokie because she had been so kind to him. And yet here were all these people, imposing their own prejudices without knowing a damn thing about us. Over the years, however, the opposition to interfaith marriage in the Jewish community has decreased considerably. When we spoke to Jewish groups after publishing *From This Day Forward* in 2000, readers would pull us aside and whisper that their children were picking non-Jewish partners. By the time we published *Our Haggadah* eleven years later, people felt much freer to speak openly about their children's choices. More rabbis were willing to conduct interfaith marriages, and several congregations where we spoke were advertising classes for non-Jewish spouses. In fact, Cokie spoke so often at Jewish events and was so popular with Jewish audiences that she was made a life member of Hadassah, a Jewish women's organization that has financed hospitals and clinics in Israel for more than a century. My Grandpa Abe, the old pioneer, would have been very proud of her.

Cokie often said that she felt "semi-guilty" about not entering politics, about turning to journalism instead of the "family business." Elected office, in her mind, was the best way to carry out the teachings of the nuns, to do "good works" in the world. She never did follow her parents' model, but in midlife she felt a calling to become more directly engaged in causes she cared deeply about. So when she ended her six-year run as host of *This Week* in 2002, she renegotiated her relationship with ABC, becoming a contract employee instead of a staff member, and that shift gave her more leeway under the network's ethics rules to become more of an advocate and activist. "I reached a certain age and realized that it was time for me to start giving back," she told Charlie Rose. "And I had preached that my whole life. I had said that women like me, who had gone directly into the workforce and had not done what our mothers had done—which was do wonderful work in the community—had an obligation to do that at some point in our lives. And that point came." Just as she was leaving *This Week*, she was diagnosed with breast cancer for the first time, and her illness lent urgency to her decision. As she told Charlie MacCormack, the CEO of Save the Children, "I've got to rebalance my time, because I don't know how much time I have left."

It turned out that she had seventeen years left, and while she was still appearing regularly on radio and television, and churning out bestselling books, her charitable work started to take up more of her time and energy. As MacCormack noted, a bright line ran through all of her volunteer efforts: "She talked about her commitment to girls and women, it was pretty central to what she hoped would be her legacy. It was clear that was really consuming to her, a passion." That passion took different forms in different settings. As a board member at the National Archives Foundation, she pushed for a major exhibit marking the one hundredth anniversary of women's suffrage in 2020. "She was the powerhouse behind the advisory group that helped ensure that we told the truth about just how painful and difficult the struggle was for women to get the vote," said the archivist, David Ferriero. "But more importantly, and she reinforced this from the very beginning, as we started talking about this exhibit, it could not just end with the vote. It had to talk about the fact that this is a struggle that continues. There are still issues that are unresolved for women's equality. That was a message she conveyed in every meeting that we had planning for that exhibit. And she was instrumental in making it as successful as it is." For many years she served on the board of the Children's Inn, which provides lodging and support for families of desperately ill children while they're being treated at the National Institutes of Health.

Cokie liked nothing more than to meet with the children and their parents, said Kathy Russell, the Inn's longtime CEO: "She just rolled up her sleeves and got in there and would relate to the kids and the families, while a lot of people were simply put off or afraid to engage. In my experience many people don't know what to say or do, so they're paralyzed. But Cokie was never paralyzed. She would ask where they were from. She would ask what their experiences have been, and people would start to open up and talk and they were just very comfortable engaging with her."

In all of her advocacy work, no organization galvanized her "passion" more powerfully than Save the Children, founded in 1919 and working today in 120 countries around the world. When Charlie Rose asked her on PBS why she had joined the Save the Children board after leaving her anchor chair, she answered: "Because they do such wonderful work, and I used all my reportorial skills and investigated various organizations. I [do] care about children—I am a mother and grandmother. But the fact is that Save the Children is efficacious. It works. And I think women especially care about that. We're not interested in wasting our time spinning our wheels. We want to do something that is going to make a difference. And Save the Children all over the world makes an incredible difference in children's lives." She traveled to a dozen countries—from Bangladesh and Vietnam to Malawi and Guatemala—witnessing Save the Children programs, and she told Rose: "Education is key. What we have learned is that if we can educate a girl, we can save a country." Mark Shriver, who runs the domestic side of Save the Children's operations, traces Cokie's devotion to the organization directly back to her religious training: "If you really believe that God is in all people, it's like, holy shit, this is really exciting because that poor Black kid in Mississippi, God's there. God's in a poor white kid in Arkansas and a poor Hispanic kid in the Central Valley. So you've got to do something, try to do something. It's being in the arena. I talked to her about that a lot and I think that Catholic social teaching had a big impact on her." Yes, Catholic teaching had a big impact, but always filtered through a woman's perspective. Carolyn Miles, for many years the CEO of Save the Children, said: "Cokie said to me one time when we were traveling that mothers will basically do whatever they have to do to make the lives of their children better. That's what I think she saw her mom do. And that's what she believed so many mothers were doing in these very difficult circumstances. That's that sentiment of 'moms just get it done,' right?"

Some of my favorite photos of Cokie were taken on her trips for Save the Children, surrounded by little kids, and Miles remembers one harrowing journey to Vietnam, where Cokie brought our daughter, Becca, along, and they were visiting a school at the top of a mountain: "It was raining, pouring down rain. And we were in two SUV-type trucks going up the mountain and it was super slippery. The road was just like a dirt road, but now a mud road and the car was sliding crazily up this road. There was a steep drop off on either side of the road, and Cokie turned around to me and she said, 'If we fall off this mountain, you're dead.' And I said, 'If we fall off this mountain, we are all dead.'" They finally made it to the top, and Cokie—who never owned a pair of jeans, or hiking boots, or athletic wear of any kind—was dressed in a skirt and leather shoes. "So she got out of the car," Miles recalls, "and as soon as she got out of the car, she sank into the mud in her little flat shoes. And she slogged through the mud, it was up over her ankles and we get to the school and she's got tons of mud all over her shoes. And there's kids running around all over the place, right? And so she jumps up and down to get the mud off of her shoes and the mud splatters all over the place and the kids start laughing. They're just laughing hysterically at this woman, with the mud all over her shoes, this crazy lady jumping up and down with the mud splattering everywhere. So then she thought, okay, this is really making them happy so I'm just going to keep doing it. So she did that awhile till the kids settled down." The area is so remote that their families have to bring the children to the school every Sunday afternoon and pick them up at the end of the week. "It takes them hours and hours and hours to walk home," says Miles, "but education is so important to these families that that's what they want to do. And I remember both Cokie and I were blown away by that school and I will never forget that visit."

On another trip to Bangladesh, a Muslim country, all the women were told they had to buy tunics that covered virtually every inch of skin before flying to a distant area and studying a program that teaches women to be home health workers. The temperature broke one hundred degrees, and the women sweated their way through many hours of visiting remote villages. At the end of the day, Cokie was asked to record a brief video about the trip, and Carolyn remembers: "She turned to me and she said, 'Are you fucking kidding me? We're going to do a film in this heat?' And I'm like, we're going to do it, Cokie, we're going to do the film. And she was like, okay. So she wiped herself down, 'cause it was really hot, and she got on camera and she did a fantastic job as she always does delivering the message of what really was going on out in this remote community and Save the Children used it for years as one of our videos."

Those trips fulfilled one of Cokie's basic precepts—live your faith every day. That faith was certainly tested by her illness, but it never faltered. When she was first diagnosed, one of her doctors was Jo Anne Zujewski, who had been raised Catholic: "I bonded with her immediately. Prayer was comforting to me, and so I figured prayer would be comforting to her. It's just the unspoken connection that you find when you meet someone like Cokie." Two years before, Jo Anne had been in Rome with her two daughters during the millennial celebration and had bought several small medals blessed by the Pope. She gave one to Cokie, she recalls, "and it meant a lot. It meant a lot more than I could have imagined." Cokie became deeply attached to the medal, even obsessed by it, wearing it on a chain around her neck every day. At times she would have to take it off for various medical tests, but when she came home the first thing she would say to me was, "Help me put my medal back on." I asked Jo Anne about Cokie's faith as her illness progressed and her doctor replied: "I think it was strong, very strong, and I think it really gave her hope. She was scared, but she also could be hopeful. I think the religion was really important, and that's why I gave her the medal. And even towards the end, I think she always maintained a strong faith. And I think that helped her accept things." Right after Cokie died, our grandson Roland, then fourteen, asked me if he could have her medal. A surprising request from a teenage boy, but of course I said yes. And he wears it every day, just as she did.

Epilogue

As I was writing this book, my sister-in-law called early one morning to say that my younger brother Glenn had died overnight after a lengthy illness. "Go back to sleep," she urged me, but as I sat there with the phone in my hand, I actually asked myself, "What would Cokie do?" And I immediately knew the answer: get up, get dressed, and go over to my brother's house, about fifteen minutes away. As I was driving there, I called my sister and told her I was following Cokie's example. You're wrong, she said, Cokie would have been there last night, sleeping on the couch. When I told my son, Lee, this story, he corrected me again. Mom, he said, would have been there for the last three nights sleeping on the couch. Perhaps, after reading this book, you too will start asking that same question: What would Cokie do?

Acknowledgments

Many of Cokie's friends and relatives were very generous in sharing their time and reflections with me. Virtually every conversation ended in tears, theirs and mine, and I joked that I needed a waterproof keyboard for my computer to finish this book, but I never could have done it without them. As Cokie was fond of saying, "thanks a million" to Avery Miller, Ariane Naulty, Annie Whitworth Downing, Anne Sweeterman Davis, Anne Reeves, Ann Mulcahy, Amy Entelis, Anita McBride, Amna Nawaz, Abbey Poze Kapelovitz, A'Leila Bundles, A. B. Stoddard, Barbara Denechaud Boggs, Barbara Fedida, Barbara Ray Stevens, Barney Frank, Becky Evans, Beth Gargano, Bill Haber, Bob Kaiser, Bob Murphy, Carol Klinger, Carole Simpson, Carolyn Miles, Catherine Allgor, Charlie MacCormack, Cinda Pratt Perlman, Courtney Kane, David Ferriero, David Glodt, David

Westin, Dee Dee DeBartlo, Diane Rowland, Donna Brazile, Dorrance Smith, Drew Altman, Elizabeth Boggs Davidsen, Emily Lenzner, George Will, Gloria Borger, Gloria Rivera, Harriett Cunningham Plowden, Holly Cowan Shulman, Ilana Marcus Drimmer, Jackie Walker, Jan Vulevich Stewart, Jane Aylor, Jean Becker, Jean Picker Firstenberg, Jim Russell, Jo Pepper Morrison Tuepker, Dr. Jo Anne Zujewski, Joe Russin, John Fitzgerald, John Noseworthy, Karen Travers, Kristin King, Larry Drumm, Kathy Russell, Laura Davis Fitzgerald, Lauren Burke, Leslee Sherrill, Lesley Stahl, Libby Miller Fitzgerald, Linda Douglass, Linda Cozby Wertheimer, Linda Winslow, Lynn Sherr, Marc Burstein, Marcia Burick Goldstein, Margo Johnston, Mark Furstenberg, Mark Shriver, Martha Raddatz, Martha Angle Walters, Mary Lou Joseph Kenny, Mary Thompson, Max Byrd, Millie Harmon Meyers, Nancy Hayward, Nina Totenberg, Phyllis Grissim-Theroux, Pia Nierman, Rini Morrison Marcus, Robert Krulwich, Robert Siegel, Robin Sproul, Sally McDonough, Sam Donaldson, Sara Just, Sonya McNair, Sr. Barbara Goergen, Sr. Carol Keehan, Sr. Clare Pratt, Sr. Joan Magnetti, Dr. Stan Lipkowitz, Steve Sigmund, Susan O'Neill, Susan Stein, Susie Holly Simmonds, Ti Adelaide Martin, Tom Bettag, Tom Brokaw, and Vicki Harte Money.

My longtime friend and agent, Bob Barnett, supported and facilitated this project with his trademark enthusiasm and efficiency. So did my wonderful editor at HarperCollins, Jennifer Barth, and her admirable assistant, Sarah Ried. This is the ninth book written by a Roberts that Claire Wachtel, our literary godmother, has helped bring into being. But it is the first aided by Rachel Faulkner, my excellent former student and current research assistant who found virtually every word Cokie ever said or wrote. And there were a lot of them. Rachel is only one of hundreds of former students who keep me nourished with their loyalty and affection.

My colleagues at George Washington University over the last thirty years have provided a professional home and personal community, and Matt Cannella guided me in establishing the Cokie Roberts Tuition Relief Fund that helped keep fifty-two students in school during the COVID-19 pandemic. I'm also grateful to Catherine Ronan Karrels, head of school at Stone Ridge, who first suggested we name the new theater on campus after Cokie. All proceeds from this book will go to those causes.

Our children, Lee Harriss Roberts and Rebecca Boggs Roberts, sustain me with meals and memories, love and laughter. So do their devoted spouses, Liza McDonald Roberts and Dan Hartman, and my six incomparable grandchildren: Regan Roberts, Jack Hartman, Cal Hartman, Hale Roberts, Roland Hartman, and Cecilia Roberts. A final word of thanks to Rosie, my chocolate Lab and constant companion, who helped fill a big empty house with her cheerful spirit.

Bradley Boulevard, May 2021

About the Author

S TEVEN V. ROBERTS has been a journalist for more than fifty years. He is the author of *My Fathers' Houses* and *From This Day Forward*, which he cowrote with Cokie. He is the chief political analyst for the ABC radio network, a professor of journalism and politics at George Washington University, and a nationally syndicated columnist. He lives in Cokie's childhood home in suburban Washington, which he and Cokie shared for forty-two years.